Seattle Public Library > REM KOOLHAAS/OFFICE FOR METROPOLITAN ARCHITECTURE

In an era of skepticism over the status of public space in the contemporary (American) city, the Seattle Public Library is a powerful statement of the the library's fundamental role as the original, and perhaps only, truly public building type. Since its opening in May 2004, it has already had profound effects in Seattle and beyond, as an urban catalyst that activates and redefines its downtown context, and as an architectural prototype whose structural and programmatic innovations offer new possibilities for creating public space in the city.

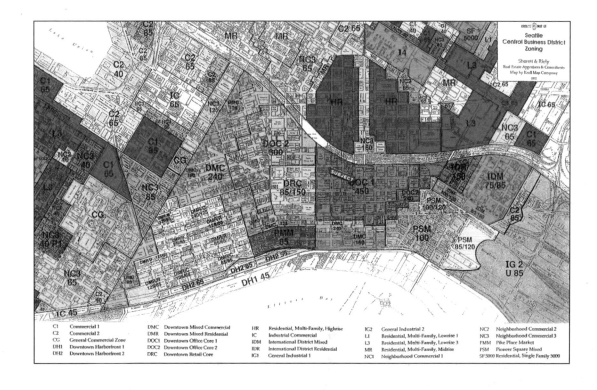

Seattle Central Business District Zoning

C1	Commercial 1	DMC	Downtown Mixed Commercial	HR	Residential, Multi-Family, Highrise	IG2	General Industrial 2	NC2	Neighborhood Commercial 2
C2	Commercial 2	DMR	Downtown Mixed Residential	IC	Industrial Commercial	L1	Residential, Multi-Family, Lowrise 1	NC3	Neighborhood Commercial 3
CG	General Commercial Zone	DOC1	Downtown Office Core 1	IDM	International District Mixed	L3	Residential, Multi-Family, Lowrise 3	PMM	Pike Place Market
DH1	Downtown Harborfront 1	DOC2	Downtown Office Core 2	IDR	International District Residential	MR	Residential, Multi-Family, Midrise	PSM	Pioneer Square Mixed
DH2	Downtown Harborfront 2	DRC	Downtown Retail Core	IG1	General Industrial 1	NC1	Neighborhood Commercial 1	SF 5000	Residential, Single Family 5000

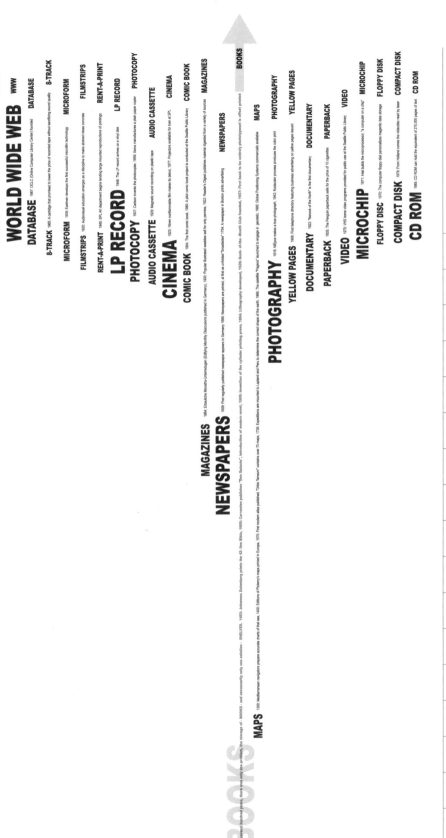

BOOKS

For several hundred years, there was only one problem... the storage of –BOOKS– and necessarily only one solution – SHELVES. 1433: Johannes Gutenberg prints the 42–line Bible. 1660's: Cervantes publishes "Don Quixote", introduction of the modern novel. 1694: Lithographic printing press developed. 1928: Books–of–the–Month Club founded. 1957: First book to be entirely photo/typeset/is offset printed

MAPS 1300: Mediterranean navigation prepares accurate charts of that sea. 1400: Editions of Ptolemy's maps printed in Europe. 1570: First modern atlas published, "Orbis Terrum" contains over 70 maps. 1735: Expeditions are mounted to Lapland and Peru to determine the correct shape of the earth. 1966: The satellite "Pageos" launched to engage in geodetic. 1995: Global Positioning Systems commercially available

NEWSPAPERS 1604: Erbauliche Monaths–Unterredungen [Edifying Monthly Discussions published in Germany]. 1609: First regularly published newspaper appears in Germany 1690: Newspapers are printed, at first as unfolded "broadsides" 1704: A newspaper in Boston prints advertising

MAGAZINES 1684: Erbauliche Monaths–Unterredungen [Edifying Monthly Discussions published in Germany]. 1900: Popular illustrated material set for only pennies. 1922: Reader's Digest publishes material digested from a variety of sources

PHOTOGRAPHY 1816: Niépce makes a true photograph. 1942: Kodacolor process produces the color print

YELLOW PAGES 1906: First telephone directory featuring business advertising on yellow pages issued

DOCUMENTARY 1922: "Nanook of the North" is the first documentary

PAPERBACK 1935: The Penguin paperback sells for the price of 10 cigarettes

VIDEO 1970: VHS home video programs provided for public use at the Seattle Public Library

COMIC BOOK 1904: The first comic book. 1980: A pilot comic book project is conducted at the Seattle Public Library

CINEMA 1923: 16mm nonflammable film makes its debut. 1977: Projectors available for loan at SPL

AUDIO CASSETTE 1932: Magnetic sound recording on plastic tape

PHOTOCOPY 1907: Carlson invents the photocopier. 1959: Xerox manufactures a plain paper copier

LP RECORD 1948: The LP record arrives on a vinyl disk

RENT-A-PRINT 1945: SPL Art department begins lending large mounted reproductions of printings

FILMSTRIPS 1920: Audiovisual education emerges as a discipline to make abstract ideas concrete

MICROFORM 1935: Eastman develops the first successful microfilm technology

8-TRACK 1966: A cartridge that promised to lower the price of recorded tape without sacrificing sound quality

DATABASE 1967: OCLC (Online Computer Library Center) founded

WORLD WIDE WEB

E-BOOK 1999: Rocket eBookTM, a hand-held device for reading web-distributed content

MICROCHIP 1971: Intel builds the microprocessor, "a computer on a chip"

FLOPPY DISC 1970: The computer floppy disk personalizes magnetic data storage

COMPACT DISK 1979: From Holland comes the videodisc read by laser

CD ROM 1985: CD ROM can hold the equivalent of 270,000 pages of text

1150 1200 1250 1300 1350 1400 1450 1500 1550 1600 1650 1700 1750 1800 1850 1900 1950 2000

The Library represents, maybe with the prison, the last of the uncontested moral universes: communal accommodations for 'good' (or necessary) activities. The moral goodness of the library is intimately connected to the value of the book: the Library is its fortress, librarians are its guardians...

As other mediums of information emerge and become plausible, the Library seems threatened, a fortress ready to be 'taken' by potential enemies. In this scheme, the Electronic becomes identified with the Barbaric. Its intangible ubiquity, its promiscuity and its uncontrollable accessibility seem to represent a loss of order, depth, tradition, civilization. In response, the language of the library has become moralistic and defensive: its rhetoric proclaims – implicitly and explicitly – a sense of superiority in mission, in social responsibility, in value...

New libraries don't reinvent or even modernize the traditional institution; they merely package it in a new way; inside, the loyalty to the book and the token acknowledgement of other forms of information are maintained. Entire potential publics are systematically alienated.

At the same time, the last decade has shown an accelerated shrinkage, if not shriveling, of the Public Domain, replaced by increasingly sophisticated and entertaining forms of the Private. Shopping has become a terminal activity of the human race, its ever expanding infrastructure relentlessly transforming the character of the urban condition itself. The essence of the Public is that it is free. Increasingly, it is replaced by accumulations of quasi-public substance that, while suggesting welcome, actually makes you pay. The Library stands exposed at its most outdated and moralistic at the moment that it has become the last repository of the free and the public.

The Library's insistence on one kind of literacy has blinded it to other emerging forms that increasingly dominate our culture, especially the huge efficiencies (and pleasures) of visual intelligence.

Unless the Library transforms itself wholeheartedly into an information storehouse and aggressively orchestrates the coexistence – under a regime of new equalities – of all available technologies and all available devices to collect, condense, distribute, 'read' and manipulate information, its unquestioned loyalty to the book will undermine the plausibility of the Library at the moment of its potential apotheosis.

Technology is not a threat, but it enables the realization of ancient ambitions – totality, completeness, dissemination, accessibility.

In any case, the anticipation of a looming conflict between the real and the virtual is moot at the moment where the two can be made to coincide, become each other's mirror image. The virtual can become the distributed presence of the library that users find confirmed in its actual site in the city.

PUBLIC LIBRARY

WORKSTATIONS 1982: An Apple II microcomputer made available at Seattle Public Library

VOTER REGISTRATION 1982: Voter registration availbel at the Central branch of SPL.

VIDEO 1981: Media and Program Services department begins coordinating the programming for public access

DISCUSSION GROUPS 1979: A series of Shakespeare discussion programs sponsored at SPL.

FRIENDS OF THE LIBRARY 1977: The Friend of the Seattle Public Library made $10,000 available for the purchase of media equipment

REMOTE ACCESS 1976: The Quick Information Center opens. 1977: Dial-a-story program begins. 1996: WWW.SPL.org goes on-line

BIBLIOTHERAPY 1971: The application of reading to the problems of emotional instability, loneliness, and alienation

ART EXHIBITS 1960: Major pieces commissioned for SPL. "Fountain of Knowledge" & "Pursuit of Knowledge". 1981: A Cable Arts festival featuring video works by local artists was held

READERS ADVISORY 1920: The reader's advisor was usually located in a quiet corner or a separate office, in contrast with the location of the reference desk which was full line of traffic. reader would come in with a topic and a course of reading was suggested

YOUNG ADULTS SERVICES 1920: Library service to this age group evoved into a supplement to the school curriculum and a provider of recreational reading, as television emerges the library has tried to redefine of service to young people.

INFORMATION DESK 1920: The separate Reference desk first appears at the Rhode Island Public Library. This increased the general component of service and well as recognizes the librian as aguide and interpreter.

LIBRARY WAR SERVICE PROGRAM 1917: Provides libraries for masses of men in the military. Most Army training camps set up libraries for draftees. Community libraries expand roles in communities by helping the Food Administration during war.

CHILDREN'S COLLECTION 1895: Most public libraries did not serve children, restricting access to those over twelve. 1900: Childrens Rooms begin to be added to Libraries. 1920: Childrens collection gain emerge popularity, which continues today

NO COST 1887: The Seattle Public Librarian's report states "we flatter ourselves that the library will hereafter be maintained forever free". 1941: Free library service given to all soldiers and sailors in the Puget Sound area. 1970: Seattle Pulic Library's first fine free day, 6,876 overdue books returned. 1973: The 10 cent charge for reserves removed.

PUBLIC LIBRARY 1854: The Boston Public Library opens as the first public library in a major American city.

EXPANDED CONCEPTION OF SERVICE 1900-1917: The American Library Association sets forth the "Library Bill of Rights". 1939: National Commission on Libraries and Information Science charged with the mission finding "an effective and affiliated library system"

"MODERN LIBRARY IDEA" 1900-1917: "Library Militant" era. General attitude that community libraries should fill a broad range roles to help solve social problems. etc. Art exhibits, education of juvenile offenders, story-telling on an elaborate scale

SPECIALIZATION 1910: The public library envisioned as "an active force, a community center striving to bring book and reader together and appeal to the entire comunity with a thousand and one activities that distinguish the modern library form its more passive predecessors"

AMERICANIZATION 1907: Fine Arts division opens at SPL. 1912: Technology department opens. 1980: The Reference department became Fine History, Goverment and Biography department. The General Reading department became Literature, Languatigesm, Philosophy and Religion

INCREASED COMMUNITY PROMINENCE 1911: First mention of the Foreign collection at the Seattle Public Library. 1916: A special assistant was put in charge of work with "foreigners". 1920: Foreign division established in the Circulation Department. 1976: Vietnamese and Arbic materials added to the collection.

ADULT EDUCATION 1920: Thanks in large part to masses of men becoming accustomed to having broad access to books during the war

GREAT BOOKS PROGRAM 1932: Early appearance at the fringe of reference service, then a distinct program with its own location and staff in the library, eventually adsorption widely in the library and community work

HANDICAPPED SERVICES 1954: American Library Association grant given to Seattle Public Library in order to experiment with the use of TV in the discussion of new books resulting in "The Challenge of Books"

TRAINING THE DISADVANTAGED 1967: The Books for the Blind program was extended to any handicapped person certified as unable to meet conventional material 1970: Young Adult department begins training for disadvantaged

INFORMATION AND REFERRAL CENTERS 1970:Information and welfare

1850   1860   1870   1880   1890   1900   1910   1920   1930   1940   1950   1960   1970   1980   1990   2000

FLEXIBILITY   Flexibility in recent libraries – SF, Phoenix, Denver – has been conceived as the creation of floors on which almost any library activity can happen. Programs are not separated, rooms or individual spaces not given unique character. In practice, it means that the bookshelves define generous reading areas at the opening, which then expand inexorably to encroach on public space. Ultimately, in this form of flexibility, the library strangles its own attractions.
A more plausible strategy divides the building in spatial compartments dedicated to and equipped for specific duties. Flexibility can exist within each section, but not at the expense of any of the other compartments... Change is possible by deliberately redefining use, rededicating compartments to new programs. (Cf. the LA library, where the main reading room was successfully transformed into a children's library.)

COMPRESSION   The fact that the contents of a simple library can be stored on a single chip, or the fact that a single library can now store the digital content of all libraries, together represent potential re-thinking: other forms of storage enable the containment of the space dedicated to real books – the other forms of reading enhance the aura of the real book.

SOCIAL ROLE   The Library has been transformed from a space to read into a social center with multiple responsibilities. A multitude of other programs has invaded the core activity of the Library, without challenging the predominance of the book. Each library today houses a proliferation of adjunct conditions that creates a conceptual imbalance: since its format has never been fundamentally adjusted to accommodate its new social role, the Library today is like a host organism overwhelmed by its parasites.

NEW EQUALITIES   Books have to share attention with other media of potent performance and attraction. Contrary to many predictions that one medium or format would kill another, we have in fact eliminated no successful modes.

hq

spiral

meeting

staff

parking

reading room

mixing chamber

living room

kids

PLATFORMS   Our first operation has been the 'combing' and consolidation of the apparently ungovernable proliferation of program and medium. By combining like with like, we have identified five <u>platforms</u> that are each dedicated to a specific cluster. Each platform is a programmatic entity that is architecturally defined and equipped for maximum, dedicated performance. Because each platform is designed for a different purpose, they are different in size, density, opacity.

The spaces in-between are like trading floors where librarians inform and stimulate, where the interface between the different platforms is organized – spaces for work, interaction, and play. (And reading.)

By genetically modifying the superposition of floors in the typical American high-rise, a building emerges that is at the same time sensitive (the slopes will admit unusual quantities of daylight where desirable), contextual (each side can react differently to specific urban conditions), iconic. Its angular facets form, with the fold of Gehry's Experience building, a plausible bracketing of Seattle's new modernity.

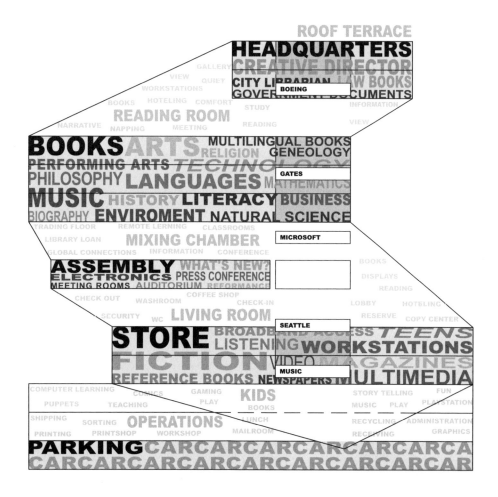

LANDSCAPE Interior / Exterior Landscape. 4th Avenue, kids, living room, 5th Avenue and Spring Street, back to 4th constitute a continuous loop of interior and exterior urban landscape.

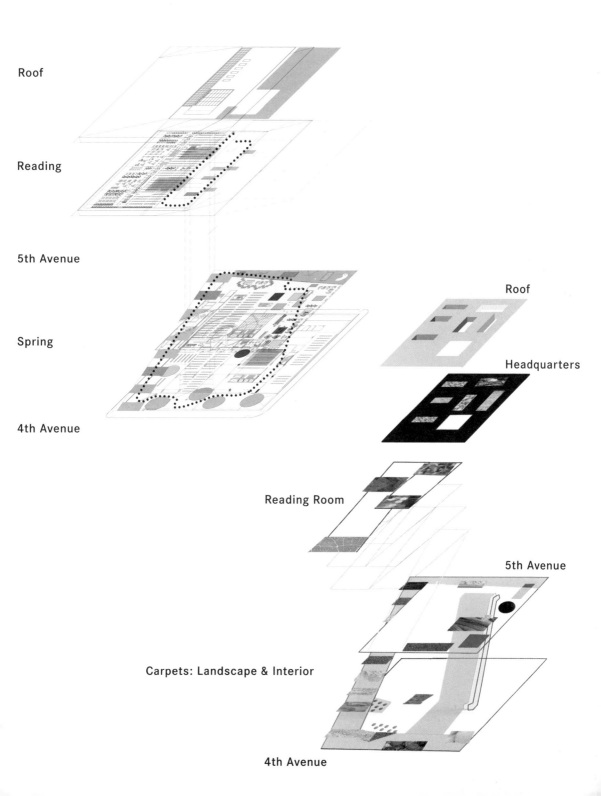

Roof

Reading

5th Avenue

Spring

4th Avenue

Roof

Headquarters

Reading Room

5th Avenue

Carpets: Landscape & Interior

4th Avenue

Reference strategy
Scenario 1: Basic orientation reference

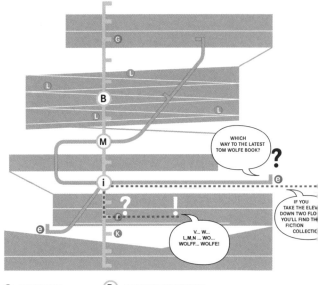

WHICH WAY TO THE LATEST TOM WOLFE BOOK? **?**

IF YOU TAKE THE ELEV' DOWN TWO FLO' YOU'LL FIND TH' FICTION COLLECTIC

V... W... L,M,N ... WO... WOLFF... WOLFE!

ⓔ	ENTRANCE INFO	Ⓑ	MAIN COLLECTION REFERENCE
ⓘ	GENERAL INFO	Ⓚ	DEPARTMENT REFERENCE
Ⓜ	MIXING CHAMBER	Ⓛ	ROVING LIBRARIANS

Reference strategy
Scenario 3: Specific study reference

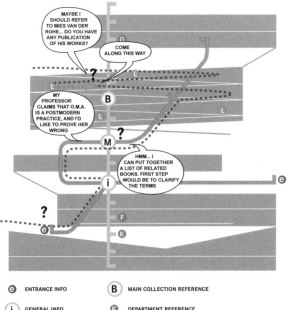

MAYBE I SHOULD REFER TO MIES VAN DER ROHE... DO YOU HAVE ANY PUBLICATION OF HIS WORKS?

COME ALONG THIS WAY

MY PROFESSOR CLAIMS THAT O.M.A. IS A POSTMODERN PRACTICE, AND I'D LIKE TO PROVE HER WRONG

HMM... I CAN PUT TOGETHER A LIST OF RELATED BOOKS. FIRST STEP WOULD BE TO CLARIFY THE TERMS

ⓔ	ENTRANCE INFO	Ⓑ	MAIN COLLECTION REFERENCE
ⓘ	GENERAL INFO	Ⓚ	DEPARTMENT REFERENCE
Ⓜ	MIXING CHAMBER	Ⓛ	ROVING LIBRARIANS

Reference strategy
Scenario 2: General information reference
(Library event)

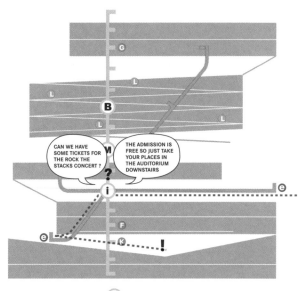

CAN WE HAVE SOME TICKETS FOR THE ROCK THE STACKS CONCERT ?

THE ADMISSION IS FREE SO JUST TAKE YOUR PLACES IN THE AUDITORIUM DOWNSTAIRS

(e)	ENTRANCE INFO	(B)	MAIN COLLECTION REFERENCE
(i)	GENERAL INFO	(K)	DEPARTMENT REFERENCE
(M)	MIXING CHAMBER	(L)	ROVING LIBRARIANS

Reference Strategy
Scenario 4: General information reference

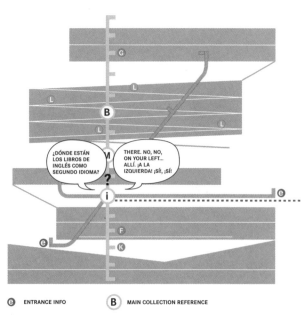

¿DÓNDE ESTÁN LOS LIBROS DE INGLÉS COMO SEGUNDO IDIOMA?

THERE. NO, NO, ON YOUR LEFT... ALLÍ. ¡A LA IZQUIERDA! ¡SÍ!, ¡SÍ!

(e)	ENTRANCE INFO	(B)	MAIN COLLECTION REFERENCE
(i)	GENERAL INFO	(K)	DEPARTMENT REFERENCE
(M)	MIXING CHAMBER	(L)	ROVING LIBRARIANS

Sunday 23 May 2004, Opening day

Seattle
p.1

Santa
Monica
p.70

Los Angeles
p.54

→ VERB

Faced with an increasing blurring of the frontiers between the physical and the informational dimension of our cities, Verb Connection explores the relation between
virtual connections – the effect of digital networks on the spaces and uses of the city
– and the persistent role of architecture in creating physical connections between
people, programs and uses. We look here into a series of projects that reveal the
unpredictable effects of the evolution of our cities, while highlighting architecture's
function as catalyst of public life and urban activity.

INTERACTIVE

In Berkeley at the corner of Hearst and Euclid, there is a drugstore, and outside the drugstore a traffic light. In the entrance to the drugstore there is a newsrack where the day's papers are displayed. When the light is red, people who are waiting to cross the street stand idly by the light; and since they have nothing to do, they look at the papers displayed on the newsrack which they can see from where they stand. Some of them just read the headlines, others actually buy a paper while they wait. This effect makes the newsrack and the traffic light interactive; the newsrack, the newspapers on it, the money going from people's pockets to the dime slot, the people who stop at the light and read papers, the traffic light, the electric impulses which make the lights change, and the sidewalk which the people stand on form a system—they all work together.

Christopher Alexander, "A City is not a Tree", *Architectural Forum*, Vol 122, No 1, April 1965, p 58.
Also in: http://www.patternlanguage.com/leveltwo/archivesframe.htm?/leveltwo/../archives/alexander1.htm

COUNTERINTUITIVE

An urban area is a system of interacting industries, housing, and people. Under favorable conditions the interplay between the parts of a new area cause it to develop. But as the area develops and its land area fills, the processes of aging cause stagnation. As the urban area moves from the growth phase to the equilibrium phase, the population mix and the economic activity change. Unless there is continuing renewal, the filling of the land converts the area from one marked by innovation and growth to one characterized by aging housing and declining industry. If renewal is to succeed and a healthy economic mix is to continue, the natural processes of stagnation must not run their normal course. But the interactions between economic and social activity are so complex that intuition alone cannot devise policies that prevent decay.

(...) From the standpoint of industrial dynamics, systems are seen as feedback processes having a specific and orderly structure. From the structure of the particular system arises its dynamic behavior. The industrial-dynamics approach to a social system organizes the growth and goal-seeking processes of the system into a computer model. A digital computer is then used to simulate the behavior of the system. The computer simulation reveals the dynamic characteristics of the system that was described in the structure-formulating stage. By changing the guiding policies within the system, one can see how the behavior of the actual system might be modified... The growth model starts with a nearly empty land area and generates the life cycle of development leading to full land occupancy and equilibrium. A variation on the model is started with the equilibrium conditions that are reached at the end of the growth cycle. This equilibrium model is used to explore how various changes in policy would cause the condition of the urban area to be altered over the following fifty years... This model of an urban system suggests that many past and present urban programs may actually worsen the conditions they are intended to improve. Promising alternative programs, addressed to the underlying causes of urban decay rather than to symptoms, suggest different approaches.

(…) It has become clear that complex systems are counterintuitive. That is, they give indications that suggest corrective action which will often be ineffective or even adverse in its results. Very often one finds that the policies that have been adopted for correcting a difficulty are actually intensifying it rather than producing a solution. Choosing an ineffective or detrimental policy for coping with a complex system is not a matter of random chance. The intuitive processes will select the wrong solution much more often than not. A complex system – a class to which a corporation, a city, an economy, or a government belong – behaves in many ways quite the opposite of the simple systems from which we have gained our experience.

Most of our intuitive responses have been developed in the context of what are technically called first-order, negative feedback loops. Such a simple loop is goal-seeking and has only one important state variable…. [But] the structure of a complex system is not a simple feedback loop where one system state dominates the behavior. The complex system has a multiplicity of interacting feedback loops. Its internal rates of flow are controlled by nonlinear relationships. The complex system is of high order, meaning that there are many system states (or levels). It usually contains positive-feedback loops describing growth processes as well as negative, goal-seeking loops. In the complex system the cause of a difficulty may lie far back in time from the symptoms, or in a completely different and remote part of the system. In fact, causes are usually found, not in prior events, but in the structure and policies of the system.

To make matters still worse, the complex system is even more deceptive than merely hiding causes… The complex system presents apparent causes that are in fact coincident symptoms. The high degree of time correlation between variables in complex systems can lead us to make case-and-effect associations between variables that are simply moving together as part of the total dynamic behavior of the system. Conditioned by our training in simple systems, we apply the same intuition to complex systems and are led into error. As a result we treat symptoms, not causes. The effect lies between ineffective and detrimental.

Jay W. Forrester, *Urban Dynamics* (Cambridge: MIT Press, 1969)

CONTINGENT

Guidebooks and maps are of little assistance in the kind of non-instrumental navigation necessitated by the urban chaos sprawling at the gates of old towns. Similarly, one only reads the user manual detailing the rules of an electronic game as a last resort. From Civilization to SimCity, the manuals that come with games are in any case deliberately laconic or obscure. The same hazardous logic based on intuition and trial and error seems to mark the discovery both of the territory city and of a new game. We seem to be witnessing the end of the traditional instructions for use. It is a widespread phenomenon; adolescents and young adults rarely read the documentation they receive with a video recorder or a computer. They prefer to discover such functions by themselves in a process that resembles DIY, a form of DIY that their elders find all the more irritating since it lacks apparent logic. The success that, in many cases, meets these rather unorthodox procedures lies in the interiorization of a new type of scheme, no longer cartographic like town plans or functional diagrams, but algorithmic, based on sequences of operations that have become familiar through testing and repetition. This kind of familiarity goes hand in hand with an approach to the environment, be it urban or technological, that is based on possible scenarios of use instead of seeking to relate it to an immediately intelligible structure.

Antoine Picon: 'Le temps du cyborg dans la ville territoire', in Les Annales de la Recherche Urbaine, no. 77, December 1997, pp. 72-77, and http://www.gsd.harvard.edu/people/faculty/picon/tempscyborg.html

UNMANAGED

Consider the Web as a construction project. (...) It is far more robust than networks far smaller, yet it was created without managers. In fact, it succeeded only because its designers made the conscious decision to build a network that would require no central control. You don't need anyone's permission to join in, to post whatever you want, to read whatever others have posted. The Web is profoundly unmanaged, and that is crucial to its success. It takes traditional command and control structures and busts them up into many small pieces that then loosely join themselves – and that, too, is crucial to its success.

David Weinberger, *Small Pieces Loosely Joined: A Unified Theory of the Web*, Cambridge, Massachusetts: Perseus Publishing, 2003, p 23.

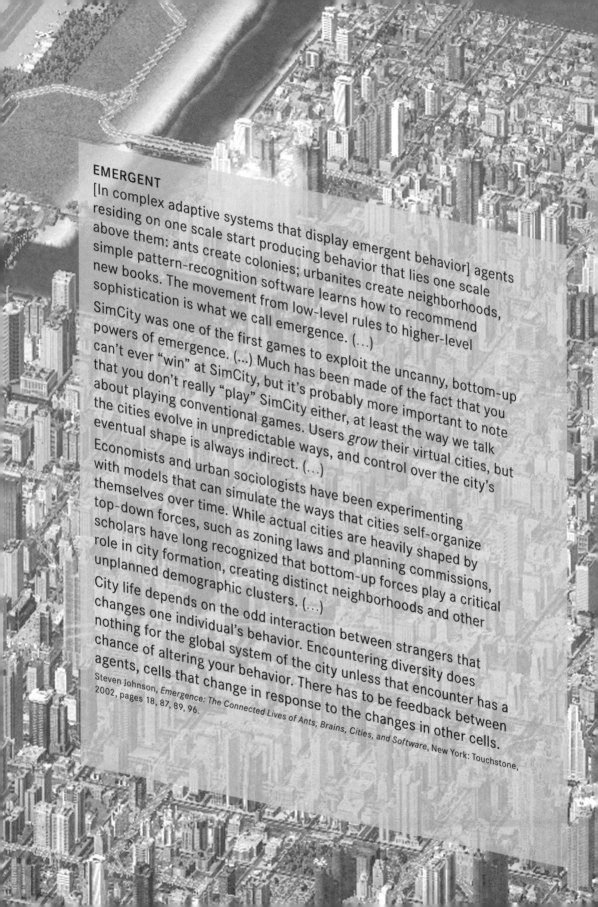

EMERGENT

[In complex adaptive systems that display emergent behavior] agents residing on one scale start producing behavior that lies one scale above them: ants create colonies; urbanites create neighborhoods, simple pattern-recognition software learns how to recommend new books. The movement from low-level rules to higher-level sophistication is what we call emergence. (...)

SimCity was one of the first games to exploit the uncanny, bottom-up powers of emergence. (...) Much has been made of the fact that you can't ever "win" at SimCity, but it's probably more important to note that you don't really "play" SimCity either, at least the way we talk about playing conventional games. Users grow their virtual cities, but the cities evolve in unpredictable ways, and control over the city's eventual shape is always indirect. (...)

Economists and urban sociologists have been experimenting with models that can simulate the ways that cities self-organize themselves over time. While actual cities are heavily shaped by top-down forces, such as zoning laws and planning commissions, scholars have long recognized that bottom-up forces play a critical role in city formation, creating distinct neighborhoods and other unplanned demographic clusters. (...)

City life depends on the odd interaction between strangers that changes one individual's behavior. Encountering diversity does nothing for the global system of the city unless that encounter has a chance of altering your behavior. There has to be feedback between agents, cells that change in response to the changes in other cells.

Steven Johnson, Emergence: The Connected Lives of Ants, Brains, Cities, and Software, New York: Touchstone, 2002, pages 18, 87, 89, 96.

Sim City

→ **VERB**

SimCity – a computer simulation game of urban development. On a vacant stretch of land you, as acting mayor, begin to mount infrastructure elements such as an electric generating station, roads, an industrial or commercial zone, a housing area, etc. When your city grows successfully large enough to collect tax revenue from its citizens, you may use the budget to build certain public facilities: police stations, schools or parks, intended to make your city better or larger, anything according to your own personal ideas. This game helps us to better understand the basic workings of a city from economic, political or environmental points of view and is used in various academic settings as an educational tool aimed at gaining insight into urban planning. Players regularly post images of 'their work' on SimCity fan sites.

background images from SS collection, www.wotax.net/SimCity/gallery
©of the game: 2003 EA GAMES™ and Maxis (Electronic Arts™ brands)

San Francisco

SimCity's interface has evolved tremendously over its lifetime. The latest version, the fourth, emulates a look that is very similar to this actual aerial photo of San Francisco, U.S. (above). It includes hyper-realistic aerial photos with fluffy clouds, as well as world famous landmarks. Chose from Stonehenge, The Parthenon, The Sagrada Familia or Seoul's Worldcup Soccer Stadium. Some landscapes assume the form of real cities like Tokyo or the partial/entire terrain of the United States.

SimCity Classic

After four years of development, SimCity is released in 1989 as the first city-planning simulation game . The game is an application of various inter-related urban planning concepts, such as traffic and zoning theories, that work together and interact simultaneously. It is now deemed a 'classic'.

SimCity 3000

Released in 1999 with various version named 'special edition' or 'XP'. Graphically, SimCity 3000 had many advances over SimCity 2000. New features included European and Asian building styles and a more nuanced ground, the color ranging from green to sand-tone. Also added were animation capabilities showing citizens and cars in transit, and further complexity in the form of garbage disposal problems.

SimCity 2000

After the success of SimCity, the 1993 release of SimCity 2000 was marked by the development of 3-D graphics, an upgrade from SimCity Classic's 16-color, 2-D interface. Players could now rotate their city and had a more complete repetoire of facilities, including: highways, a subway system and varied structure types, like a zoo or statues. An additional kit allowed players to design their own buildings, customized to fit personal taste, with public reaction recorded in virtual newspapers.

SimCity 4

In addition to the part of 'mayor,' the fourth version of SimCity included two more 'God modes,' where players now had the power to affect natural disasters or ground topography. The 'My Sim mode' controlled the population of Sim People in the city. Players could choreograph at various scales, from the micro-detail of the individual, to the mega-scale of natural elements. Graphics were further refined to include realistic touches in the form of construction sites with welding sparks or drifting clouds.

44

→ VERB

SimCity has no fixed recipe for success nor targeted end-point. Players watch their cities grow, monitoring their development, problems, and occasional disasters, induced by certain user decisions. This image is a screenshot of one player's creation – a continuous farm-to-city landscape. Individual players have unique visions of their ideal city: a megalopolis with millions of inhabitants, an eco-friendly green city, or a facsimile of a real world city; all are sustainable within the SimCity program .

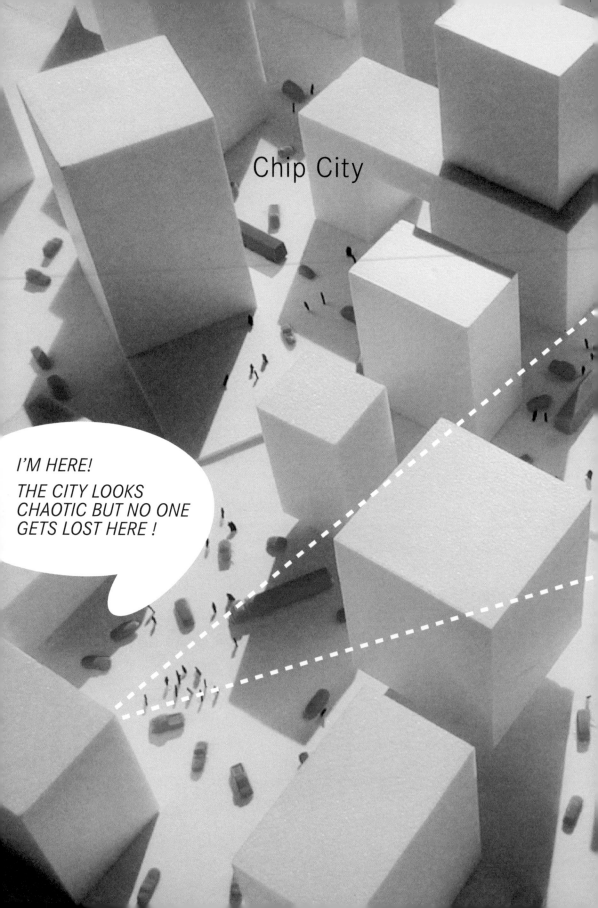

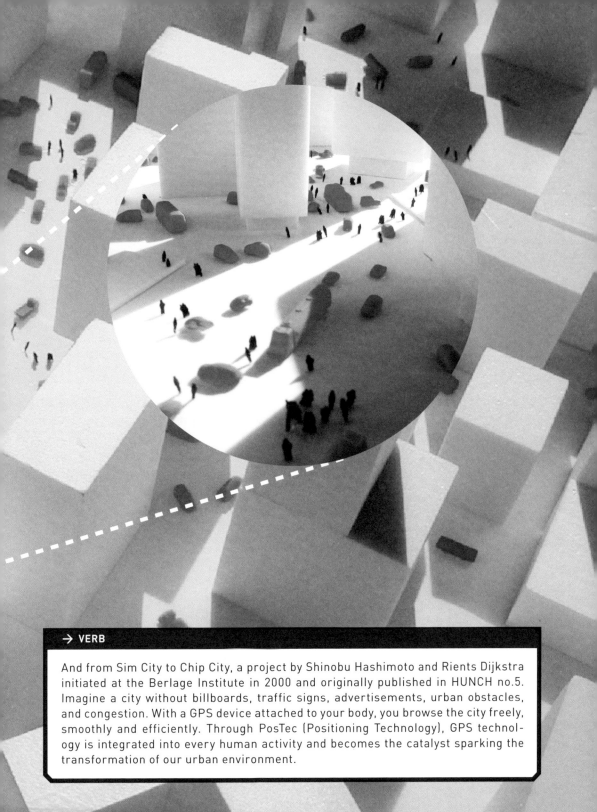

→ VERB

And from Sim City to Chip City, a project by Shinobu Hashimoto and Rients Dijkstra initiated at the Berlage Institute in 2000 and originally published in HUNCH no.5. Imagine a city without billboards, traffic signs, advertisements, urban obstacles, and congestion. With a GPS device attached to your body, you browse the city freely, smoothly and efficiently. Through PosTec (Positioning Technology), GPS technology is integrated into every human activity and becomes the catalyst sparking the transformation of our urban environment.

Chip City > Shinobu Hashimoto and Rients Dijkstra

A small part, a piece, a fragment - these are the elements that make up the whole. Sometimes a small part can transform the whole; fragments become giants - catalysts for change. Our designs for buildings and cities are influenced by our beliefs about a society's future performance. How appropriate are these beliefs? Is it safe to simply extrapolate? Imagine a small device that tracks the exact position of all people and objects on the globe, in real time, with pinpoint precision. The following pages relay a thought-experiment about such a device's influence on the city of the near future.

GPS (Global Positioning System) technology, originally developed by the military in the early 60's for purposes of precision weapon delivery, is now being applied in everyday life, as a navigation tool. If your body, your car, your boat, or your plane

WHAT WILL GPS DO?

PRIMARY: **POSITIONING**
PRINCIPLE: *Knowing where I am*
the place is / the thing is / anytime
any weather / anywhere

PRIMARY: **TRACKING**
PRINCIPLE: *Knowing the velocity*
Measuring the movement of people
and things

PRIMARY: **NAVIGATION**
PRINCIPLE: *Finding your way*
Getting from one location to another
Getting information surround the position

PRIMARY: **MAPPING**
PRINCIPLE: *Creating maps of the world*
Managing infrastructure
Maintaining and updating

PRIMARY: **MEASURING**
PRINCIPLE: *Centimeter level survey*

Photos / Trimble

carries a GPS device, its position on the globe can be pinpointed to within 20 meters of accuracy. The world stays the same; the way we find our way around it is made more convenient. The way traffic works will change beyond comprehension. Cars will know the position, direction, and speed of other cars. Road signs, road markings, crash barriers, traffic lights, speeding, car accidents, parking problems, taillights, and getting lost will all have disappeared.

More motion but less collision. More information but less signage – fixed signage, that is. The promise of GPS is that the sign will be miniaturized, internalized, personalized. If people, buildings, and objects all carry miniature Positioning Technology (PosTec) devices that can communicate among themselves, will life simply become easier?

The remarkable thing about GPS is that it delivers information depending on your position. PosTec will soon be the catalyst for human activity. As the capabilities of the individual increase, so will the transformation of the urban environment.

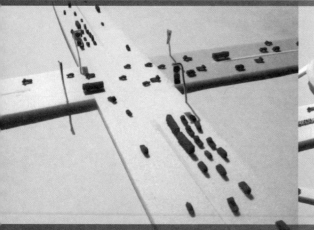 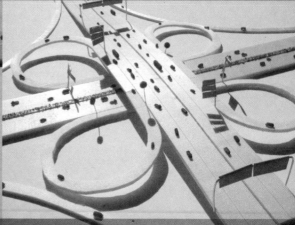

THE EVOLUTION OF THE HIGHWAY!

MODEL 1   Safety requires slowing down at the crossing. Traffic rules dictate intersection behavior. Traffic signals, pavement, traffic rules and indicators help to prevent collision.

MODEL 2   The need for speed gives rise to space-consuming chunks of concrete. Large numbers of cars move in all directions simultaneously. Big curves let you change directions safely and smoothly. A lot of the space required remains empty and useless.

THE EVOLUTION OF THE CITY!

MODEL 1   Lined up along the infrastructure. Commercial activity dominates the ground level on main streets. Many areas at ground-level, facing the main street, are considered more profitable.

MODEL 2   Position is value, size is impact. Since the ground level position is fully occupied by commercial programs, density increases vertically. The building's façade, and signage on the building surface are conceived to attract attention of pedestrians and car drivers.

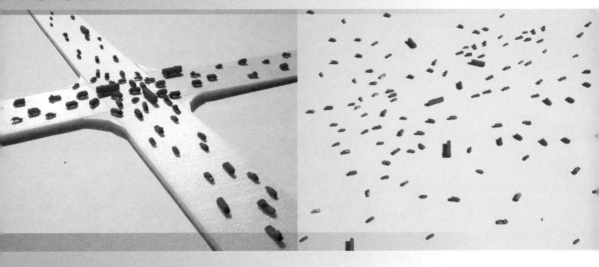

MODEL 3 Concrete and signage are soaked up by PosTec. The layout of the road is determined only by the necessary capacity. Simple PosTec calculations result in a speed and a course that will make you cross the intersection without stopping.

MODEL 4 Return to innocence - linearity lost. The road loses its linear form. Earth is cut up into 'motion space' and 'obstacle space'. Under PosTec surveillance, people and public events will coexist safely and efficiently.

MODEL 3 The individualization of the screen - hierarchy lost. More and more information is transmitted through screens. Large signs are inert and mass-oriented, small screens are agile, personal and wearable. Physical hierarchy, as a means of organizing a city, becomes irrelevant.

MODEL 4 The street concept loses all relevance. With PosTec, the quality of location and land value are determined by points of access (parking, public transport) and clustering around 'good spots'.

CHIP-CITY ROTTERDAM!

CHIP-CITY TOKYO!

Los Angeles, 2004

Ether
The One Wilshire Building

AUDC / Robert Sumrell and Kazys Varnelis

LOS ANGELES AND THE THEOLOGY OF ETHER

In *Empire*, Antonio Negri and Michael Hardt describe the new world order created by the global spread of capital and communications technology. If national governments are withering away under the deterritorializing and liquefying forces of capitalism, Negri and Hardt claim that a new sovereignty is emerging, a transnational order they call Empire. This diffuse network supplants the old imperial model of centre and periphery, replacing it with a placeless network of flows and hierarchies.

Empire is not ruled by one country, one people or one place. Instead, its force emanates from the global planetary network itself. Imperial sovereignty functions through three tiers that serve as checks and balances on each other while extending its power to all realms: monarchy, aristocracy and democracy. These forms of sovereignty correspond to the Bomb (US military superiority and nuclear supremacy), Money (the economic wealth of the G7), and Ether (the realm of the media, culture and the global telecommunicational network). Although these tiers are placeless – any momentary fixities are quickly destabilized by the deterritorializing nature of Empire itself – Hardt and Negri suggest that 'new Romes' appear to control them: Washington DC for the Bomb, New York for Money and Los Angeles for Ether.

Of these three forms of power, the one that concerns us here is Ether, the historically most advanced form. Ether has an anesthetic quality. It separates the mind from the body, and reduces the dominance of physical sensation while maintaining the consciousness of the patient. Under the spell of its influence, the most intimate and cherished of all physical space, that of the body itself, can be assaulted at will. The use of ether to reduce pain in childbirth was originally banned by the Church, which argued that the suffering of original sin should not be relieved.

Los Angeles is the centre of production for ether. Hollywood, as both a mythical place and a mode of production is the telematic inhaler for the rest of the world, a sponge so soaked and saturated with ether that it can anaesthetize the entire world. Now that we have Los Angeles, we no longer need other cities. Los Angeles has been designed as a giant stage set, ready for broadcast. As a generic background, it can be exported to any location.

THE PALACE OF THE EMPIRE OF ETHER

If the empire of ether were to have a palace, it would have to be the 39-storey One Wilshire tower in downtown Los Angeles. Constructed at the apogee of modernism by Skidmore Owings and Merrill, One Wilshire unequivocally declares that form follows function. Perhaps the worst building SOM ever designed, excusable only as a product of the provincial San Francisco office, One Wilshire appears to follow only two guiding principles. First, in order to create a visual identity, One Wilshire was designed as a tower. Second, One Wilshire's window areas were maximized to provide light and views for the occupants. Throughout the design, expression of any form, including the expression of structure, was eliminated as superfluous. One Wilshire is the pure modernist building. Its neutral grid lacks symbolic content, making it a tower without qualities.

One Wilshire embodies the desire of the bourgeois metropolis to appear at all cost. Awkward in proportions and off-axis with regard to Wilshire boulevard, One Wilshire's only feature is height, incessantly affirming the value of the land beneath it. But this one symbolic affirmation would also be the building's downfall.

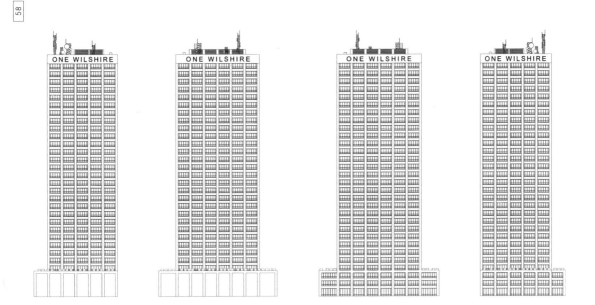

THE FLUID METROPOLIS

In his essay 'The Fluid Metropolis' (*Domus* 496, March 1971), Andrea Branzi tracks the downfall of the skyscraper and the urban core. He observes that 'the skyline becomes a diagram of the natural accumulation which has taken place of capital itself'. Once capital takes over 'the empty space in which [it] expanded during its growth period,' now that 'no reality exists any longer outside of the system', the skyscraper's representation of the accumulation of capital becomes obsolete. Branzi concludes that the horizontal factory and the supermarket – in which the circulation of information is made optimum and hierarchies disappear – would replace the tower as the foundational typologies for the fluid metropolis.

Branzi is, of course, correct. The increasingly horizontal corporation, organized along super-Taylorist and cybernetic principles of communicational efficiency, constructs low, spreading buildings for its offices in the suburbs. Consequently, in Los Angeles as in other cities, the congested vertical urban core began to empty. One Wilshire's once beneficial vertical signification of 'office building' and 'valuable real estate' began to get in the way of its own economic sustainability. By the mid-1980s, One Wilshire was obsolete.

In 1992, however, a new opportunity presented itself and One Wilshire's height came to its advantage. With the deregulation of the telecommunications industry, MCI required a tall structure on which to install microwave antennas

that would be in close proximity to the SBC (formerly Pacbell and prior to that AT&T) central switching station at 400 S. Grand downtown.

One Wilshire was ideal for this task. Seeing a friendly environment close to the central switching station, competing long-distance carriers, ISPs, and other networking companies began to lay fibre-optic cable to One Wilshire. As fibre technology has improved, the microwave towers on top have dwindled in importance – they are now used by Verizon for connection to its cell-phone network. At the same time, the vast amount of fibre running in and out of One Wilshire allows telecoms the possibility of creating direct peer-to-peer connections in the structure, thereby avoiding charges imposed by linking through a hub.

TELECOM HOTELS CREATE IMMATERIAL CULTURE

Because space in One Wilshire is at such a premium, companies run conduits to adjacent structures. Over a dozen nearby buildings have been converted to such telecom hotels, providing space to telephone and Internet companies seeking locations near the fountain of data at One Wilshire. This centralization of information defies predictions that the Internet and new technologies will undo cities. Neither, however, does it lead to a revival of downtown in classical terms. The buildings are valuable again, but largely uninhabited. Still, if one of the reasons for the downfall of the American downtown is the slowdown in transportation and wear on infrastructure created by congestion, the emptiness of the streets in Los Angeles's telecom district ensures that this will never be a problem.

One Wilshire stands as a continuous demonstration of the phases of the metropolis and the current state of the post-metropolitan world. One Wilshire demonstrates that the new functions of the city do not need a shape of their own but rather are repelled by that possibility. The transformation that One

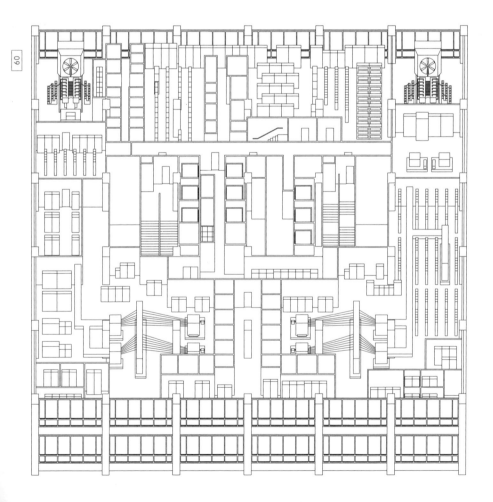

Wilshire underwent from its construction in 1966 to its transformation in 1992 paralleled the transition from material to virtual reality during the Cold War. With the full development of the post-metropolitan realm and the corresponding global saturation of material production, we enter the world of immaterial culture. One Wilshire demonstrates the transformation of the city into a system of objects and the importance of the network in that system.

UGLY AND ORDINARY

For the most part, One Wilshire is an ugly and ordinary building, akin to the now classic post-modernist retirement home, Guild House. In designing Guild House, Robert Venturi and Denise Scott Brown decided to avoid the monument and instead build a structure more appropriate to the banal demands of modern life. Cut-rate detailing and low-cost prefabricated elements made Guild House a stark reminder that modernism won its battle not because of ideology but because it was cheaper to build than neo-classicism.

Like Guild House, One Wilshire is simply a neutral shell lacking any aesthetic gestures. There is no reason to think that Bunshaft wouldn't have called One Wilshire 'ugly and ordinary' as well. It was constructed at almost the same time as

Guild House and shares many of its features. It too is a decorated shed and has its own second-rate sign. Banal modernist lettering across its façade announces the presence of 'One Wilshire' to the rest of the city. Although the antennas at One Wilshire originally had a purpose, they are now just as superfluous as the ornament once crowning Guild House, empty symbols of a retired modern technology. But One Wilshire goes a step further than the decorated shed: its signage is obsolete from the start so it will never need to be removed. The building's real address is actually not One Wilshire, but 624 South Grand. An unbridgeable gap between signifier and signified, between form and function opens up at One Wilshire.

The fact that this architecturally meritless structure is also the most valuable real estate in North America only confirms that the role of the building as a producer of effect or meaning is obsolete.

WILD SIGNS

Where Guild House was a home for the elderly, One Wilshire is the home in which we dwell telematically. Just as the elderly watched television in Guild House as a way of checking out of the weariness of life, we check into the global space of telecommunications in order to escape the dead world of objects. In both cases, however, the desire is to leave behind this world of material goods for something more pure, and to escape our responsibility to them by submitting to something greater.

Real objects are quickly known and classified. They give themselves up too easily. Like potential lovers, once they are purchased, objects become dead to our desires, lifeless pieces of junk. The telecommunicational realm promises that the spirit can finally part from flesh and exist fully in a world of electronic

images. These images are seductive because, circulating endlessly in an ethereal world, they cannot be possessed. We can fantasize about having such images to no end without ever feeling the disappointing responsibility of ownership.

Before late capitalism, objects had meaning because they were necessary but scarce. In our affluent society, however, objects are overabundant, becoming merely components within a system of exchange without any clear use-value to determine their price. The very basis of late capitalism presupposes the delinking of currencies from the gold standard or any other guarantor of value. Today money proliferates wildly even as it means nothing.

There is no longer a clear logic to the system of capital. The dot-com boom, Beanie Babies and vastly inflated real estate values are all based on mass delusion. Value itself does not come out of any deeper truth but is constructed by temporary notions and mass delusions. This is a defensive measure for capital, so that massive run-ups in markets and unprecedented collapses can occur without any real consequence to the larger economy.

SYSTEM OF OBJECTS

As the logic of our daily lives becomes more and more removed from the direct consequences of our actions, objects are marketed and sold for their symbolic values alone. A teapot by Philippe Starck costs more because of its styling, even though it doesn't really work. But even the styling doesn't really matter, only Starck's name as a marker of value counts. Physical objects carry value only at moments of exchange: the moment they become so desirable that you want to purchase them and the moment that you can no longer tolerate their presence and want to get rid of them.

The increasing role of telecommunications and computers in everyday life does not do away with objects, far from it – in immaterial culture physical objects proliferate endlessly.

We still feel the need to own objects, even if the gratitude of ownership is fleeting. The on-again and off-again emotions we have about our objects confuse us, leaving us bewildered and lost. But physical objects will always ultimately repel us because they cannot satisfy our desire for self-negation, our desire to lose ourselves in their world. So it is that our love for objects is routinely replaced by a deep hate. We sell our possessions relentlessly on eBay but still they accumulate, contributing nothing to our lives. Every day more debt, more things, less joy.

We will never find a release from the need to own. Even if we can't sustain the gratitude of ownership, we purchase goods to validate our identity and diversity as individuals existing outside of this media web. But more than that, in submitting ourselves as willing slaves to our world of useless objects, we hope to become as disposable to them as they are to us today. If we cannot join their world, we dream of a new equality: being as ethereal and meaningless to them as they are to us. We hope that we will be allowed to leave this material world and dissipate in ether. And yet, as conflicted beings, we also hope that one day our objects will invest in us the same animistic beliefs with which we invest them. This is not our nightmare, it is the achievement of an utopian dream, presence without purpose or responsibility: a slacker response of ambivalence and helplessness. The dream of immaterial culture is revenge on the world of objects.

A GIANT STOCK EXCHANGE

Within immaterial culture, consumer goods lose their natural meaning and become fully abstracted as empty forms, ready to be filled with a variety of meanings that we apply to them depending on context. Immaterial culture makes possible a system of consumption beyond cynical reason in which even the most sinister or foul objects can be desirable. Whoopi Goldberg collects negrobilia, Bruce La Bruce films gay porn in which Nazi Skinheads ejaculate onto the cover of *Mein Kampf*, and Andrea Dworkin, an anti-porn activist, writes pornographic rape fantasies.

These objects are wild signs, free-floating signifiers that carry opposed meanings simultaneously. All objects are now wild signs. Unable to represent anything specific themselves, they instead become part of the mechanism of circulation, which has become a goal in and of itself. Money, as Hal Foster observes, the guarantor of value, has become the ultimate wild sign. Gold is locked away at Fort Knox, too heavy to move while the value of currency is tied to abstraction and desire. With nothing underwriting it except Derridean 'différence', the economy is sustained only because of the continued inevitability of circulation in the network.

THE METROPOLIS IS COMPLETE

If, as we have already established, the new is now simply another aspect of the already-existing, all we can do is recycle old things in phases to make them newly desirable commodities again, just as One Wilshire was recycled into a citadel for immaterial culture. Supply and demand emerge out of what is already lying around.

The difference between immaterial culture and the material culture that preceded it is that not only have none of the physical elements of society changed, they will never need to be changed again. The metropolis is complete. Only our relationship to the elements of the world around us is freed of permanence and keeps moving.

Either things don't mean anything anymore, or we don't, or both. Although nothing has a universal meaning or a lasting value, objects still convey provisional meanings and attain temporary values created on the fly, often for very short durations. For a month a Beanie Baby is worth $1,000. The next month it is worth $3 again. This doesn't mean that anything goes. Objects can still only function within a system. The empty promise of objects is precisely what allows them to remain vital. There is no longer a fixed natural state of identity or being. All that is left is desire and the craving for its impossible satisfaction.

Value is now a commodity in and of itself, regularly sought out and consumed. All objects and all people are members of a giant stock exchange, not as investors on the floor, but as flickering numbers running across a banner, some rising, some falling, but always moving up and down.

THE VIRTUAL AND THE REAL

The virtual is generally perceived as a drive against the spatial or physical world. Nevertheless, the virtual world requires an infrastructure that exists in the physical and spatial world. Though ether is formless, it has to be created. Its production requires an enormous amount of physical hardware and consistent expertise.

Because of this, ether is primarily produced at nodes and locations where key players can meet and collect in front of and behind cameras and computers. Massive telecommunicational urban hubs like One Wilshire and their radial networks make the virtual world possible, and firmly ground it in the concrete cityscape. Once this raw data of ether is created, it has to be stored and organized through stable control centres. These control centres, filled with row after row of servers, generate an enormous amount of heat and require vast cooling systems with multiple back-up power units in order to function without interruption. Constant monitoring of these systems is vital as interruptions affect the entire system. Once the data has been collected, it has to be distributed outside the building. Fibre-

optic cable is currently the most effective way of transmitting large quantities of data out of the building into the rest of the world. This cable is expensive to lay and requires a significant negotiation of civic, private and even international property as when fibre crosses national boundaries. Telecommunication companies cannot afford all of these investments individually and have opted to pool their resources at a single location providing connectivity close to the transmission source. Through One Wilshire, virtually all of the global market leaders share a physical investment on the West Coast. Being 'plugged in' is their literal need, not just an abstract notion.

THE BECOMING UNREAL OF THE REAL
One Wilshire is tied to this physical location, it undermines the concept of an autonomous virtuality, revealing instead the simultaneous importance and abandonment of the physical world. In short, all of media and all of virtual life may be transmitted through non-physical technologies, but it is not possible to catalogue or store it without ties to storage and material culture. One Wilshire is an unimportant building without any physical presence or ability to signify its function as the palace of the empire of ether, yet it is crucial. One Wilshire is the unreal exposing and making real of the unreal.

Individuals also long to become virtual and escape into ether. It is through this physical apparatus that Hollywood stars, celebrities and criminals obtain another body, a media life. Neither sacred or living, this media life is pure image, more consistent and dependable than physical life itself. It is the dream we all share: that we might become objects or, better yet, images. Media life can potentially be preserved for eternity, cleansed of unscripted character flaws and accidents – a guaranteed legacy that defies ageing and death by already appearing dead on arrival. The idols of millions via magazines, film and television are disembodied, lifeless forms without content or meaning.

But the terrifying truth is that, although a media image may be eternal, like

Michael Jackson, its host is prone to destruction and degradation. Data itself is not free of physicality. When it is reduplicated or backed up to file and stored via a remote host it suffers the same limitations as the physical world. It can be erased, lost and compromised. The constant frustration of CDs, DVDs and hard drives is that they don't last forever, and all data is lost at once. Up to 20% of the information carefully collected on Jet Propulsion Laboratory computers during NASA's 1976 Viking mission to Mars has been lost. The average web page lasts only a hundred days, the typical life span of a flea on a dog. Even if data isn't lost, the ability to read it soon disappears. Photos of the Amazon Basin taken by satellites in the 1970s are critical to understanding long-term trends in deforestation but are trapped forever on indecipherable magnetic tapes.

CAPITAL AND MILLENNIUM

That the dot-com and telecom busts occurred in the first year of the new millennium is no accident. Those who participated and invested in these busts acted irrationally but not without reason. Like the followers of the Heaven's Gate cult and those who hoped that the year 2000 or, better yet, a Kubrick-esque 2001 would mark the end of all things, they were just desperate to believe that the end was near. The process of investing in Pets.com was a matter of giving oneself up. Borrowing on margin to invest not only the entirety of one's pension in Akamai or Worldcom but to generate a life-crushing debt as a by-product as well was a form of voluntary slavery.

The pundits were mistaken; it was not that we all hoped to get out of the boom before it failed, it was that we wanted to be part of its failure and to feel its destruction. The greatest disappointment of the dot-com crash of 2000 was its failure to bring about the promise of the dot-com era: the end of all things.

Today, Rem Koolhaas and other members of the post-avant-garde maintain that architecture should do nothing more than embody the flows of capital. Instead of enslaving itself to capital, as it does now, and instead of fulfilling the master-slave dialectic to become capital's master, as it always wished to be under modernism, architecture now decides to end the game and achieve oneness with capital.

ETHER IS THE MEDIUM OF SELF-NEGATION

If achieving a state of oneness with capital is architecture's fantasy, what better place for this to happen than at One Wilshire? If architecture is to become capital, it will do so by becoming ether. This is only possible when architecture loses all sense of intrinsic value and enters into a pure system of exchange. Technology allows architecture to dissociate itself from any specific interior condition and to become one with ether. Through symbol libraries and the magic of the .dxf import command, it has become possible for architectural plans to reproduce at will. The toilet rooms from Frank Gehry's signature building, the Guggenheim Museum at Bilbao, can be copied onto a CD-ROM by an intern to endlessly re-appear in schools of architecture worldwide, their first role in life irrelevant and forgotten. In this light, the prevalence of the computation-intensive BLOB in the academy is revealed as the product of fear, a desperate attempt to reintroduce the hand and slow down architectural production just at the moment that it threatens to proliferate wildly, allowing architecture to become pure ether.

One Wilshire has no such fear. Created before the dawn of computer-aided design, it transcends architecture as pure diagram and pure Idea. Endlessly replicable, there is no limit to its potent reach. It is the architectural realization of Hegel's Spirit itself. One Wilshire is a masterpiece of terror. It is an architecture of pure self-negation, simultaneously real and virtual, visible and unseen. One Wilshire is the palace for the empire of ether.

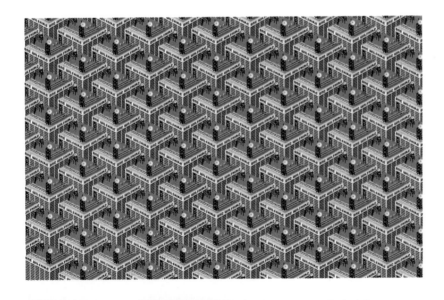

Santa Monica, 1950

Network-Building: The RAND Corporation, Santa Monica

Introduction > MICHAEL KUBO

The RAND Corporation, established in 1948 to preserve the scientific brainpower collected by the United States military during World War II for the new strategic imperatives of the Cold War, has long been known as the epicenter of strategic military thought in the 1950s and 1960s, an institution whose mission was "to think the unthinkable" – the rational assessment of nuclear war and its consequences. While its most important early contributions to fields like national security, space technology, computing and the Internet have been widely publicized, one of the first and most important works of research to emerge from RAND (short for Research and Development) remains almost unknown: the Santa Monica building in which the company has been housed since 1953, a two-story modernist structure whose design quietly prefigures many of the key concepts of contemporary architectural discourse. Ten years before the Berlin Free University and Albert's project for Jussieu, the headquarters of the RAND Corporation is both the archetype of the mat-building – the dense, extensive horizontal structures projected by architects in the 1960s – and the built diagram of its analogue, the distributed network, one of the cornerstones of the information age that would emerge, significantly, from within RAND's own halls more than a decade later. A direct outgrowth of the interdisciplinary research culture of the institution, the building is today a forgotten monument to the development of an objective, research-driven architecture, a built manifesto of design method whose non-descript qualities belie its status as the ancestor of a line of architectural research that has only recently taken on renewed importance. Never publicized by its architect or its client, today the building is on the verge of destruction, its deliberate anonymity so total that its potential value for the discipline is still unrecognized. The RAND building is best considered not as architecture but as a form of built research, a problem-solving exercise in the rigorous organization of a center for the production of innovative thinking. In 1950, in anticipation of the project to build a permanent headquarters for the corporation, John Williams, the head of the mathematics department, wrote an internal memo in which he systematically developed the basic principles for a new building. Starting with a simple question – "Why are we building a building?" – Williams arrived at the premise "that RAND represents an attempt to exploit mixed teams, and that to the extent its facility can promote this effort it should do so. This implies that it should be easy and painless to get from one point to another in the building; it should even promote chance meetings of people." This implied the need for a dense, compact structure that would generate maximum connectivity between all parts of the building, yet preserve sufficient light and air to all offices. This double imperative led Williams to explore the theory of regular lattices ("a fascinating subject"), a line of investigation that immediately suggested the ideal configuration of the building: a regular grid of circulation paths or hallways around enclosed exterior patios, where the average distance between any two points (as a function of the overall length of the hallways) is reduced as the density of the grid increases. The optimal size of the lattice would then be determined by the dimensions of the site, balancing the decrease in average distance against the reduction of patio space as the lattice becomes more complex.

Moving from the diagram to its translation into the scale of a building, Williams identified a further key to the solution, discovering an explicitly architectural method to improve on the abstract structure of the lattice: "it might be that, in view of the climatic conditions here, we could throw all or most of the halls out of the building. The patios could be surrounded by porches onto which the office doors would open [to] provide cover against the rain on those three or four happy days; otherwise, one could cross the patios from office to office." By absorbing a percentage of the circulation grid within their perimeters, a minimum dimension for the patios could be maintained even as the number of paths increased, additionally reducing the average distance between offices even further by allowing the patios to act as shortcuts within the lattice.

The translation of this brief – an analysis that already constituted, in effect, a schematic design for the building – into a physical structure was entrusted to H. Roy Kelley, a Los Angeles architect primarily of upscale suburban residences whose previous work had also included the camouflage of factory buildings during World War II for the Douglas Aircraft Company (where RAND began as a research division), designing their rooftops to look like suburban California towns, complete with fake roads and houses. Built from 1953 to 1957, Kelley's project conforms precisely to the solution outlined in Williams's memo: a two-story, 5-by-3 lattice of hallways surrounding eight open patios that serve as both circulation and ventilation. All offices have casement windows that open to the exterior, and the final building even adopts the typical dimensions assumed by Williams in his analysis: 26 ft wide sections, with 6 ft wide corridors and 9x13 ft, 18x13 ft, or 18x18 ft offices for one, two or four people. The RAND headquarters as built is thus the almost literal construction of a mathematical diagram, designed by means of an abstract, rational method according to purely organizational criteria: the logical solution of a problem in graph theory at the scale of human occupation.

The resulting building was, by all accounts, every bit as productive as Williams had hoped for, a machine for catalyzing interactions – and ideas. According to Paul Baran, the electrical engineer who invented the concept of the distributed network while at RAND, "It's very difficult to get people with such different skills – physics, social sciences – to connect. But RAND was the most productive damned place I've ever seen." It is no surprise that Baran's innovations took place here, since the building itself is consciously designed to function as a distributed network: a dense, redundant grid of circulation with maximum connectivity between parts. The goal behind its organization, to increase the number of possible paths between any two points, is a literal expression of the fundamental principle of the distributed network: multiplying the number of routes a message can take to its destination to ensure transmission in case specific paths are destroyed. Both building and network are structured to maximize communication, and both systems are formulated on the basis of graph theory, the mathematics of nodes, paths and connections.

If the building's design grew out of the characteristics of the institutional culture at RAND, it also played a crucial role in shaping that culture. It is telling that the term "think tank", originated in Britain in World War II, was first used in the US to refer to RAND's operations – a description of both its mission and the environment in which its work took place, a hermetic container where advanced research could be conducted safely. RAND thus offers the paradox of a highly controlled, top-secret environment organized to maximize the potential for chance interactions. The external secrecy of the institution was matched by the looseness of its internal dynamics: researchers were not given mission assignments, and the building was open twenty-four hours to allow the staff to roam the halls at any time of day. (John Nash, one of the most famous mathematicians to work at RAND, was especially renowned for wandering the building's halls; fellow mathematicians, seeking to introduce their problems to him, would contrive to step into his path in order to attract his attention.) The holistic approach generated by the building's layout, where researchers in theoretical disciplines like math and physics and were in constant contact with work in applied fields like economics, psychology and engineering, would eventually anticipate the most influential result of RAND's investigations for contemporary thought: the idea of systems analysis, a research method based on the study not of isolated problems, but of the total systems in which actions and decisions occur. First used in the analysis of military operations, this

methodology would come to permeate all the work done at RAND after the 1950's. The systems analysis approach would ultimately be responsible for RAND's most important innovations, from some of the defining concepts of Cold War strategy (e.g., Albert Wohlstetter's concepts of "fail-safe" and the "second-strike" capability, and Herman Kahn's theory of "mutually assured destruction", or MAD) to advanced technical research that would establish the basis for the development of intercontinental ballistic missiles, satellites, modern computing (the Johnniac computer was developed at RAND to meet the increased computational requirements of research based on systems analysis), and the Internet.

Today, both the expansion of the RAND Corporation and the intended anonymity of its architecture have condemned the original building to destruction. Soon to be abandoned for a new headquarters next door whose curvilinear forms are meant to symbolize the "non-linearity" of the research process – an aesthetic expression of scientific method designed only to represent possibility, not to generate it – the current building will soon pass into legend. Forever liberated from its physical presence, perhaps all that will ultimately remain of the RAND building will be its deep structure, the conceptual architecture that underlies its physical organization: an abstract diagram and the rigorous analytical procedure by which it was developed. One hopes that will be legacy enough.

From: J.D. Williams
To: RAND Staff
Subject: Comments on RAND Building Program
Date: 26 December 1950

These notes are going directly from dictation to vellum, so as to save a little time; it follows that I am not prepared to defend their organization, the grammar, or anything else about it that looks weak in the light of day.

We suddenly find ourselves in a rather advanced state on our building program. It has changed from a vague gleam in our eyes, which was the steady state for several years, to a state where the building site is looking pretty firm and the architect is about to walk in the door. It's a little like Korea: our preparations for the event, while far from negligible, leave something to be desired.

We have discussed this subject among ourselves only a little, and usually at times when we felt we should be doing something else. We have had time to sound off extreme ideas, ranging from an eight-story obscenity at Hollywood and Vine (with a supermarket on the first floor), to whatever the character had in mind who wanted to be able to hear a cricket. I feel that the subject deserves some thought and time, that we should try to reach a meeting of minds, and that now is the time to do it.

If it does no more than provide a basis of disagreement, I thought it would be valuable for somebody to set down some of the facts and fancies that we hold. With these as a starter, I hope we will add and subtract items until we arrive at a set of essentials which cannot be compromised, at a set of desirable entities, and a set of things to be avoided. This memo is not organized along those lines.

Why are we building a building? Aside from some intangibles, such as a feeling of and a look of permanence, that it would give us, the motivation must come from some or all of the following:

> 1. better location;
> 2. a better organized facility;
> 3. better space for individuals.

If it is the need for these that drives us, we had best make sure – in fact, damn sure – that we get them in gobs. For this is going to be a very permanent and very expensive operation; it will be a long time before we can second-guess, and we could do a lot of interesting and important research, and/or stake some of our people to advanced training, with the money. While it is inevitable that compromises will have to be made all along the line, it is important that we not get winded by the details: we must be prepared to abandon the project even at a late date, if the potential benefit gets too low.

But excluding both tents and marble, there is probably a factor of two floating around in the costs. A rural site might be purchased and developed for under two hundred thousand dollars, and a building, which would satisfy our present needs, might be built for as little as half a million. On the other hand, an urban site might cost over half a million, and a building estimated to satisfy our ultimate needs could cost a million. It is my guess that a building on an urban site would tend to be more expensive than one on a rural site, simply because it would have to make up by artifice some of the values inherent in a rural site, such as quiet.

We have given no thought for a long time, so far as I know, to the question: how should a facility for RAND be organized? Several years ago Frank and Arthur Raymond gave some thought to it in connection with the Douglas loft. They made some sketches of an office layout comprising concentric rings of offices with the senior people being concentrated toward the centre. While the particular design they explored was suited only to the Douglas loft, or some similar dungeon, the underlying motives still should attract us; namely, that RAND represents an attempt to exploit mixed teams, and that to the extent its facility can promote this effort it should do so.

This implies that it should be easy and painless to get from one point to another in the building; it should even promote chance meetings of people. A formal call by Mr X on Mr Y is the only way X and Y can develop such a tender thing as an idea – the social scientists have taught me to use X and Y in that bawdy manner. If the interoffice distances are to be kept reasonable, the building must be compact. It need not be circular; a square is often a good substitute for a circle, and even a rectangle is not bad, if the aspect ratio does not get out of hand.

The argument which favours having a compact structure does not extend to space-filling solids. Inter-floor travel is undesirable, but chiefly because so little of it is done. When coupled with inter-building travel, it almost vanishes. As current examples, I hazard that Lloyd, Jimmy and Gene rarely see each other except at formal staff meetings, and their divisions must maintain contact by the Christmas list.

Because of the absolute side of our organization, it doubtless is not feasible to have it arranged so that Elaine in Electronics and Ethel in Publications have optimum physical communications, nor is it especially useful that they have it. But it would be worth a lot if people like Harris and Kahn, Specht and Marcum, Dresher and Wiley, Ansoff and Clement, etc., were as accessible to one another as Goldy and I.

The compactness criterion, unfortunately, runs headlong into another set of values, namely, those that concern the characteristics of a desirable office.

I believe that the qualities that are more desired are, approximately in the order of importance:

1. Privacy;
2. quiet;
3. natural light;
4. natural air;
5. spaciousness.

There is room for argument on some of these. Working from the weak end, it could go without saying that, because space in the sense of building footage is an expensive and rare commodity, that spaciousness must be obtained mostly through illusion – this is the place where the architect must make with the magic. And there are some sports (in the Mendelian sense) such as Goldy, who like to live in tubes and take their light and air from bottles, and there may be some people who have to be seated in rows in order to keep each other awake. Almost everybody likes it quiet.

While we undoubtedly require several office types for single occupancy as well as several for multiple occupancy, it is fairly important that the desirability of offices, within a type, be fairly constant throughout the building. Otherwise those who get the less desirable ones will be unhappy.

I believe that almost all of our requirements can be satisfied, and in a reasonably priced structure, if we have enough land. Since we have a strong internal reason for building compactly, the argument in favour of a substantial piece of land is not that it is desirable to spread out the building. The principal function of land is to provide insulation and isolation, and spaciousness. Insulation from noise, isolation from distractions and from the public gaze – my present office windows are high to begin with and then the bottom section is frosted – just so that people waiting for buses, or otherwise loitering, cannot participate in my meetings.

One of the really interesting, and pressing, questions is: can we put up a building on a piece of land as small as that opposite the City Hall and still get approximately what we want? On my own part, there are times when I think we just can, and other times when I think we just can't.

Just to have something concrete to think about, I invented some typical offices and structure to go with it, and have been trying to fit on to that piece of property. For purposes of illustration, I will describe them briefly; but let me say that I appreciate that others will have ideas, and doubtless better ideas on sizes and arrangements – I am only prepared to shed blood from my veins in defence of these; not artery blood.

But first, recall that RAND now has about four hundred and fifty people, of whom about three hundred are office dwellers; the rest live in Washington, machine rooms, and open areas, or they are nomadic, such as the guards and janitors. These people live in about two hundred offices; about one hundred of these are singles; about seventy are doubles – correction, about one hundred and ten of these are singles – about seventy are doubles; and about twenty are occupied by three or four persons. I guess that in a new building there would be fewer of the last and more doubles.

I consider three office sizes, for purposes of exploration. These were – these are – nine by six and one-half, nine by thirteen, and eighteen and one-half by thirteen; inside dimensions, in all cases, I require that the first have one window and that the other two have two windows. The first is suited only to single occupancy, the others, single or alterable or for two occupants.

I hypothesized six-foot width for hallways. Offices of these types can be accommodated in a building element, or wing, or section, thirty-four feet wide, outside measure, allowing six inches for each wall. The hall can be central with 9 x 13 or 9 x 6' offices on both sides, and the hall would be at one side where 18' x 13 offices on both sides, and the hall would be at one side where 18' x 13 offices prevail. I have played with this a little, and it is pretty flexible and efficient. This model at least serves to give some ideas about total building footage required.

The first peek at the problem suggests that our present size of organization and the size of the urban properties that are being considered, a one-story structure is infeasible. This is strengthened if we take into account the possibility that RAND may grow. I have, therefore, considered the elements of RAND in two categories, research and non-research, in the hope that at least the research people could be kept conveniently together on one floor. This does not quite get us off the hook; however, because future growth of RAND, if it occurs, would presumably be growth of the research arm, principally. Therefore, the building plan should be flexible enough to encompass (say) another 150 research people. The 9 x 13 offices mentioned earlier are a convenient unit. In terms of them, I estimate that our present needs for research offices and associated facilities (e.g. conference rooms) are 200 units. Similarly, the non-research functions (e.g. numerical analysis, publications, business administration, etc.) seem to require about 150 units. In the future the research elements might require 300 units and the non-research perhaps 200 units. If you treat the 9 x 13 unit as occupying 13 x 13' of building space (thus including the walls and half the hall), you get 175 square feet per unit. This indicates that the present needs for research and non-research are like 35,000 and 25,000 square feet, respectively, and that these may eventually change to 50,0000 and 35,000, respectively. Using a standard building section, 26 feet wide, the research staff would need about 1,350 linear feet of that structure and the non-research staff would need about 1,000 linear feet of such structure; eventually these might change to 1,900 and 1,300.

Now having some idea about how much space we needed, and of a way of packing it into a building section in a manner to provide light and air for all concerned, I was then ready to festoon the landscape with this stuff in some useful manner, if possible.

Judging from modern buildings I have seen, a popular way of spreading stuff around is to arrange it like the bone structure of a fish: a central structure with wings jutting out at intervals on both sides of the skeleton. It may be a useful design for us, if we have enough land. But for the parcel which we are now considering so seriously, the fish skeleton eats up the available space very fast; and it is not the best design for inter-office travel.

I was therefore led to try a system of closed courts or patios and became involved in the theory of regular lattices, which is a fascinating subject; the square, the figure eight and a hierarchy of more complicated designs.

As one rough measure of the utility of such designs, from our special point of view, I have taken the average distance between offices, measured along the grid – i.e. the halls. With any intelligent arrangement of our people, we can do better in practice than these average distances, but they still offer some information which is pertinent to us. I insert here a little table which gives the average distances for various simple lattices, expressed as a percentage of the total length of all the halls in the building. I also exhibit a picture of one of the lattices. The last column (S) in the table shows the overall size of the lattice. We note that the average travel distance decreases as the lattice becomes complex, that the decrease is most noticeable for the square lattices and that the decreases are particularly noteworthy in the first two or three steps. For example, in a nine-patio lattice (i.e. a 4 x 4), the average distance is 10 percent of the total length of halls, as compared with 25 percent in the case of the simple square. Also, the size of the building as measured by its side S is half as great as that for the square.

Average Distance Between Points in Lattice
(measured along lattice lines expressed as a percentage of the total length of all lattice lines)

$\mu_1 = 3 \quad \mu_2 = 4$

No. of vertical lines (μ_2)	No. of horizontal lines (μ_1)				
	2	3	4	5	S
2	25	-	-	-	25
3	19	14	-	-	17
4	17	13	10	-	12
5	15	12	9.6	7.5	10

S = length of side of the square lattices (as percentage of all lattice lines)

Of course, you have to watch it a little when you begin to translate the lattice into building structure. The building sections have finite width (twenty-six feet in my model), which reduces the width of the lattice openings; the people who live there, and who were so happy initially, will begin to notice it if the patios shrink too much. What the useful minimum is, perhaps our architect can tell; perhaps our psychologists can assist him. A little playing with this will convince you that it is possible to put us on a fairly small piece of land – maybe. For example, even our hypothetical future research organization, requiring nineteen hundred feet of halls on this model, could be fitted on and around a nine-patio system, measuring two hundred and sixty-four feet on a side; on the three hundred and forty-four feet deep property opposite the courthouse, this would permit a forty-foot set-back on front and rear. The patios would be like fifty-three feet across. I don't know what you would do with the non-research fractions of RAND. Of course, a second story would put over two-thirds of the ground floor. Such second story space might be regarded as less desirable than the first story space, and it might depreciate the first story space: for example, the patios might have to be larger to be equally desirable what with all that overhang (correction – what with all that structure rearing up about it).

There is another way to make the patios somewhat larger, and which would make small ones more tolerable – and which would moreover reduce the average interoffice distance below that of the lattice: it might be that, in view of climatic conditions here, we could throw all or most of the halls out of the building. The patios could be surrounded by porches onto which the office doors would open. The porches would provide cover against the rain on those three or four happy days each year: otherwise, one could cross the patios from office to office. These small sheltered areas would not be windy.

My guess is that if a multiple patio scheme were artfully done, it would develop that 'outside offices', in the normal sense, would rank low in popularity for they wouldn't be less quiet and intimate; in fact, the vista from them would be filled with unrewarding objects such as automobile traffic and the rear of the Elks Club. Of course, the number of outside offices diminishes as the lattice becomes more complex.

Later: After seeing the above, I was tempted to fix it up a little. But reason prevailed: the way it is, those who disagree with a point will have to guess whether it's me they disagree with, or my secretary, who often construes my 'woulds' as 'wouldn'ts', etc.; conversely, they may find me biting their flank just when we seem to have reached harmony.

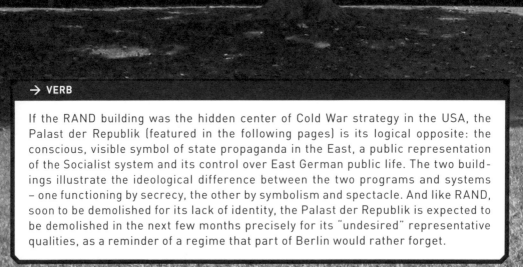

→ VERB

If the RAND building was the hidden center of Cold War strategy in the USA, the Palast der Republik (featured in the following pages) is its logical opposite: the conscious, visible symbol of state propaganda in the East, a public representation of the Socialist system and its control over East German public life. The two buildings illustrate the ideological difference between the two programs and systems – one functioning by secrecy, the other by symbolism and spectacle. And like RAND, soon to be demolished for its lack of identity, the Palast der Republik is expected to be demolished in the next few months precisely for its "undesired" representative qualities, as a reminder of a regime that part of Berlin would rather forget.

Berlin, End of the 20th century

→ VERB

The transformation of this site on Berlin's Island of Museums stands out for its central position in the urban fabric and its significance as a representation of state power. The Palace of the Republic, built in the 1970's on the foundations of the Palace of the Prussian Emperor and the medieval city walls, survives today next to the Berlin Cathedral and the reconstructed Lustgarten as an empty relic of the GDR. Although the reunified German parliament voted for the demolition of this symbol of the socialist regime and the reconstruction of the Prussian Palace, the current uncertaintly created caused by lack of funding has become fertile ground for new proposals in the definition of public space.

Foyer

The demolition of the Prussian Castle (Stadtschloss) gave place to the vast Marx-Engels-Platz, conceived simultaneously as the culmination point of all popular and military parades and as the forecourt of a new government tower to be constructed on the opposite bank of the Spree river. Twenty years later, the administrative center was redefined into a new civic center that combined the most representative institution of the republic, the Volkskammer (People's Chamber), with a wide range of venues for popular events, including auditoriums, restaurants, a bowling alley, and a discotheque.

For a thorough documentation on the building and the Stadtschloss site, see Thomas Beutelschmidt, Julia Novak, ed., *Ein Palast und seine Republik*, Berlin: Verlag Bauwesen Huss-Medien, 2001.

PALACE OF THE REPUBLIC, BERLIN. GERMANY

Location: Berlin-Mitte, Schloßplatz (formerly Marx-Engels-Platz). Architects: Heinz Graffunder with Karl-Ernst Swora, Günter Kunert, Manfred Prasser, Wolf R. Eisentraut, Heinz Aust. Construction: 1973-1976. Dimensions: 182 x 90 x 32m. Gross floor area: 103,000 m². Main functional areas: 1. Volkskammer (People's Chamber) of the German Democratic Republic (GDR) (35 x 29 x 11m, 540 seats + 240 on balcony for spectators); 2. Foyer and public halls with restaurants, discotheque, bowling center and 200-seat auditorium on 4th floor; 3. Großer Saal o Big Hall used for conventions, concerts and balls, with movable walls and decoration (maximum height 18m, 5,000 seats); 4. Basement with storage, kitchen and machine rooms. Also known as: House of 1,000 windows or Honecker's lamp store.

Palast der Republik, 2004

Main Auditorium

Foyer and entrance

1950: Demolition of the Hohenzollern-Castle after a decision of the ruling Socialist Party. **April 1973:** Council of Ministers of GDR decides construction of the palace. **Architects:** Heinz Graffunder, Karl-Ernst Strowa. **April 1976:** Opening of the "Palace of the Republic". The palace is divided into the sections: "People's Chamber" (GDR parliament), "Lobby" and "Great Hall"(convention hall for 5000 people). While the parliamentary chamber is rarely active, the Palace is popular as a public cultural venue. The building is a primarily a multi-functional Superbox, including thirteen restaurants, cafés and bars; a theatre, bowling alley, discotheques, etc. With its 15.000 visitors per day it is the most frequently visited location in Eastern Berlin's centre. **March 1990:** Constitution of the first freely elected parliament of East Germany. **August 1990:** The "people's chamber" votes to dissolve the GDR and join the Federal Republic of Germany. **September 1990:** The palace is closed due to asbestos contamination (sprayed asbestos was used as a fire protection for the steel structure). **October 1990:** The government of the Federal Republic of Germany becomes the new owner of the Palace. **1990-2004:** Sealed box: the building remains closed for four-teen years. **1998-2001:** Stripping of interior to expose structural shell in order to remove asbestos (overall cost: approx. 70 million euros). **November 2000:** Federal Government establishes the "International Commission of Experts 'Historical Centre'" consisting of fif-teen German, one Austrian and one Swiss member. **April 2001:** Final report recommends demolition of Palace and reconstruction of new building ('Humboldt Forum') on the footprint of the destroyed castle; the programme of the Humboldt Forum is envisaged as a combina-tion of two existing Berlin libraries, the scientific collections of the Humboldt University and the relocated collection of Non-European Art (estimated cost: 670m Euros); an interim cultural use of the existing structure is recommended. **July 2002:** The German Parliament (Bundestag) formally votes for the demolition of the Palace and the reconstruction of the main historical facades of the Hohenzollern-Castle around a future building. **July 2002:** A second expert group 'Schlossareal' (Castle Area) is set up to develop detailed spatial and financing concepts for new building. **March 2002:** The local initiative consisting of studio urban catalyst and diverse cultural users create pressure group to campaign for a tempo-rary use. **November 2002:** The pressure group organises exhibition of ideas, 'Zwischen Palast Nutzung' displaying possible temporary use scenarios and initiating public debates. **March 2003:** Formal constitution of 'Zwischen Palast Nutzung' as a non-profit organisa-tion and beginning negotiations with Federal Government about a cultural interim use. **May 2003:** Asbestos removal from contaminated sites is completed. **July 2003:** 'Zwischen Palast Nutzung' and local tourist association conduct guided tours through the palace-shell reopening of the building for the first time since 1990 to thousands of visitors. **October 2003:** The official expert group 'Schlossareal' (Castle Area) recommends a two-year-lasting moratorium for building plans in view of current economic depression. **November 2003:** Bundestag votes again for the demolition of the Palace. The site of the Palace designated as grassed park area until funds for a new building can be found. **March–June 2004:** Commercial exhibition of reproductions of the Chinese "Terracotta army". **June 2004:** Annual Congress of the Federal Association of German Industries (Bundesverband der deutschen Industrie – BDI) held inside the appropriated Palace. **July 2004:** Final signing of temporary use contract limited to three months (official contract holder is the cultural venue Sophiensaele Berlin and the Hebbel Theatre). **20. August–9. November 2004:** VOLKSPALAST – period of temporary cultural use opens the building with over 40.000 visi-tors to date. **September 2004:** The original plan to demolish the Palace of the Republic by the beginning of 2005 is cancelled due to irregularities in the tendering process. **October 2004:** the Federal Minister for Culture, Dr Christina Weiss, agrees to postpone the opening of the Palace for cultural use until mid 2005. **16–17. October:** FUN PALACE Berlin 200X – international conference.

Architects as agents

Studio Urban Catalyst
Philipp Oswalt, Philipp Misselwitz

BACKGROUND   The Palast der Republik, opened in 1976, was one of the most important and ambitious public building projects in East Germany, housing the GDR parliament as well as several major cultural venues, clubs, bars, restaurants and conference facilities. In 1990, after only fourteen years of use, the structure was vacated on grounds of asbestos contamination, and currently the building remains unused – the period of vacancy already exceeding the duration of use. During a six-year and costly asbestos removal programme, the building was stripped down to its core structural elements, a steel frame and pre-cast concrete elements, and became a gigantic space of rough and evocative beauty located in the very heart of the city, hidden behind its largely intact brownish mirror façade. Throughout the last decade the future of the Palast has been the subject of a heated and polarised debate. In 2002, by a slim margin, an international expert commission and the German parliament eventually voted in favor of demolishing the Palast and of constructing a new building that would integrate elements of the imperial Prussian castle that had formerly occupied the site; this plan would have an estimated cost of 668 million euros. Today, the future of the site is still unclear. Although it was determined that a new 'Humboldt Forum' would occupy the property in order to house the state-owned non-European collections, the science collection of Humboldt University and the central library of Berlin, the scheme has neither funding nor a credible architectural solution[1]. During a recent session held in October 2003, the German parliament conceded that the initial plan would be postponed until after the current economic recession and it is widely believed that a lack of public funding could postpone construction for another five to ten years. This waiting period is exemplary for the failure of traditional planning in conditions of crisis: whilst the final form of the project has been fixed, the key questions of finance, client and program remain unanswered. Moreover, the almost ideological fixation with the building's final image seems to block any sense of realism and appropriateness of the project and makes a pragmatic discussion of alternatives nearly impossible. In a para-doxical decision to conceal the inability to act and the lack of a clear concept, the German Parliament voted to invest a further 20 million euros into the demolition of the existing Palast. Thus, the site would remain indefinitely a large, grassed over area.

1. See: http://www.bundesregierung.de/artikel-,413.535194/Abschlussbericht-der-Arbeitsgr.htm
   http://www.bundesregierung.de/-,413.534455/pressemitteilung/Kulturstaatsministerin-Weiss-E.htm

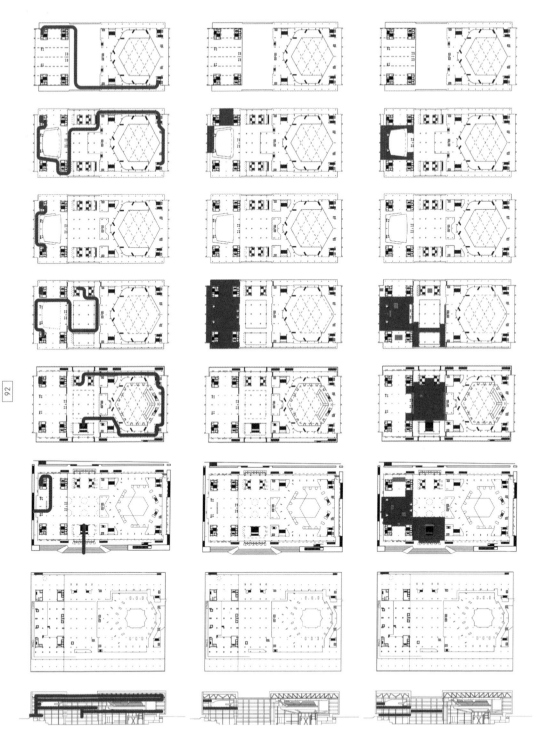

Visitors   Sophiensäle   DTM

THE IDEA OF TEMPORARY USE   The idea for the temporary use of the existing, structural remains of the Palast der Republik was proposed in the spring of 2002, at the same time that Studio Urban Catalyst became involved in the project. The Senator for Culture, Adrienne Goehler, and the architectural critic Bruno Flierl had responded to expressions of interest by several cultural institutions, such as the Berlin Sophiensaele (off-theatre) and the Staatsoper (State Opera), but the idea remained without a clear and realistic concept. As we contemplated the possibility of getting involved as architects, we had to concede that the situation was rather absurd: there was no client, the building was already there and there was no money to pay for its necessary appropriation. In response to this situation we developed a multi-track approach. As a first step, we began to identify and contact initiatives and institutions that had voiced an interest in temporary use and to inform other groups that would likely be interested. Six groups eventually joined us in regular meetings, forming a loose network in which each of the initiatives pursued a different programmatic idea, representing a spectrum that seemed realistic and appropriate to us: concerts, opera, art installations, exhibitions, discotheque, as well as sport and youth culture. In parallel, we began to develop ideas for necessary improvements of the pre-existing structure, guided by the belief that the installation of temporary uses would cost a fraction of the officially published ten million euro estimate. At that time, access to the well-guarded building was nearly impossible, the owner (the Ministry for Construction and Built Environment) was unavailable, and updated plans of the stripped interior of the building were non-existent. In order to move forward, we needed the help of those politicians that had expressed their support for the idea in the past. In April 2002, we persuaded the planning authority of the Mitte district to host a large meeting, which for the first time, assembled representatives of the owner, the planning authority and potential users. As a result of a rather difficult and inconclusive discussion, we were given the mandate to lead a smaller working group in order to develop a feasibility study based on the following objectives:

> To develop an architectural solution that addressed the issues of fire escape and safety and to propose a basic infrastructure for a wide spectrum of temporary use scenarios;
> To focus existing ideas to form a coherent concept;
> To propose a management structure that would assume all responsibility for the implementation of the proposal;
> To identify realistic strategies for the financing of the necessary initial investment and operation costs.

Over the following period of 8 months we developed a concept based on the following premises:

> Only a limited selection of spaces should be appropriated for temporary use in order to reduce costs (two alternative scenarios were considered);

> Minimizing the necessary interventions to the structure in accordance with the provisional character of the building, designed for a transitional time-frame of 2-3 years (with the option of extending this period in accordance with the progress of plans for a new building), before the building's eventual demolition;

> Ensuring that implementation costs incurred by the owner of the building (the Federal Republic of Germany) remain little to none – no revenue (e.g. rent) is expected (temporary users take on running costs of the building);

> Laboratory: the interventions would ensure a maximum spectrum of possible uses, with the belief that cultural events help to reenergize a public discussion about site's future while acknowledging the deep attachment to the Palast still felt by many East Germans.

TEMPORARY USE GOES PUBLIC With the help of expert advice, the spatial concept and necessary interventions to the structure were refined with an estimated cost of 1.3M € – less than 15% of previous renovation cost estimates and a fraction of the cost for new development. But whilst the necessary preparatory work had been done, relations with the owner remained difficult. Requests for meetings were left unanswered. Even the initial support of several politicians turned cautious and half-hearted. In order to move forward with the project, we realised that direct negotiations with the owner would not be given serious consideration unless we managed to build strong public support in the background. In November 2002, a 5-day public exhibition was organised in an abandoned governmental building adjacent to the Palace of the Republic. For the first time, the feasibility study

and an exemplary selection of programmatic ideas were presented to the wider public. Several thousand visitors attended the opening event of the exhibition, and the presence of over 100 journalists at the preceding press conference confirmed the widespread media interest. The almost unanimous support for the initiative in the national press, TV and radio during the following weeks generated a favourable backdrop for the start of negotiations. The German Finance Ministry, by then the official owner of the building, accepted the viability of the proposed measures but refused to be directly involved in the management of the temporary use project. The necessity of securing an appropriate partner, with limited legal viability, led to the re-constitution of our initiative as the legally recognised, non-profit society ZPN "ZwischenPalastNutzung" (UseBetweenPalaces). Studio Urban Catalyst continued to be a vital engine within the framework of this organization. The formalisation of the loose network of users and agents (suc), enabled ZPN, as a potential lease-holder, the ability to manage the constant inquiries and declarations of interest posted by an extremely varied user community.

DIRECT ACTIONS   As negotiations for a temporary-use tenancy agreement stalled, ZPN devised a new strategy of small actions, hoping to generate a 'Trojan horse' effect. In partnership with the event organiser Partner für Berlin, the building was opened again for the first time to the general public within the framework of limited guided tours, again accompanied by major media coverage and public attention. Studio Urban Catalyst, in partnership with the stage-design specialist Mediapool, devised a series of low-budget interventions that secured a path through the central part of the building and remained in place even after the tours had finished. In September 2003, the secured area could therefore serve as a basic infrastructure for 'musical walks' – a sound performance by Christian von Borries and the Brandenburg Philharmonics – the first cultural event,

which again attracted several hundred visitors. It is hoped that the continuing strategy of accumulating small-scale interventions will maintain a high level of public interest and convince the owner of the feasibility of temporary use as a viable option, which would generate a modest income and cover some of the costs of security and maintenance. Simultaneously, the curatorial concept was refined in discussions with renowned curators Hans Ulrich Obrist (Paris), Boris Ondreicka (Bratislava) and Hannah Hurtzig (Berlin) and presented to the public on December 19, 2003, along with a revised concept for the appropriation of the former Palast-Foyer – a much cheaper and more realistic option based on an external and potentially mobile fire escape system of temporary scaffoldings and an internal mobile sprinkler system that can be placed in areas of high fire risk.The curatorial concept '1000 day' formulated, with an ironic relationship to the former building structure, three platforms for the programme: entertainment, politics, communication. A set of seven rules were devised in order to regulate the interaction of actors, e.g. limit the size of projects by time and space, ensure a dynamic change over time as well as refreshing impulses from the outside. The building would become an open source project, highly inclusive and non-hierarchical.

VOLKSPALAST   Three years after the start of the initiative, a three month, temporary-use contract was finally signed. The Palace of the Republic was reopened as 'Volkspalast' (people's palace) on August 20, 2004 as a multi-purpose space. Initial investment was secured through private sponsorship in order to meet safety standards and fire regulations. The diverse program consisting of concerts, art installations, music festivals, theatre performances, club events, sport and leisure events, water city and labyrinth, exhibition space or conferences has attracted over 40,000 visitors. The projects constitute a temporary laboratory testing new forms of public space, interaction and communication

with the intention to generate close proximities of different, otherwise segregated social and cultural groups. Volkspalast was closed on 9 November because the current lack of heating facilities made the continued use of the structure impossible.

PROSPECTS   Despite the bleak prospects for the realisation of the planned Humboldt Forum and the apparent success of the interim use, the German government insists on the rapid demolition of the Palace in accordance with the original parliamentary vote. The recent postponement of demolition until autumn 2005, due to irregularities in the tendering process and the possibility of hosting the 2005 World Championships in Beach Volleyball in front of the building (July 2005), may have unexpectedly created the opportunity for a second period of temporary use (possibly May –September 2005). However demolition, lasting twelve to fifteen months (2005/6) at an estimated cost of twenty million euros, remains high on the agenda and will yield no more than a grassy field, marking the footprint of the pre-existing building for an indeterminate period of time. Before seeing a substantial improvement in the alarming economic situation or the taking of another parliamentary vote, it is unlikely that this or any future government would commit public funds for a new building, thus eliminating the possible elaboration of a potential programme and subsequent architecture competition. Through the vehicle of a well-known and symbolic building, the discussion of alternative approaches to urban development was given a unique platform that could provide impetus to future projects and encourage the acceptance of temporary use as an integral part of urban development. For us as architects, the involvement of Studio Urban Catalyst as an agent and facilitator of the temporary use initiative is an experiment of lasting value – a potential model for a new territory of action for architects, acting less as builders and more as urban agents.

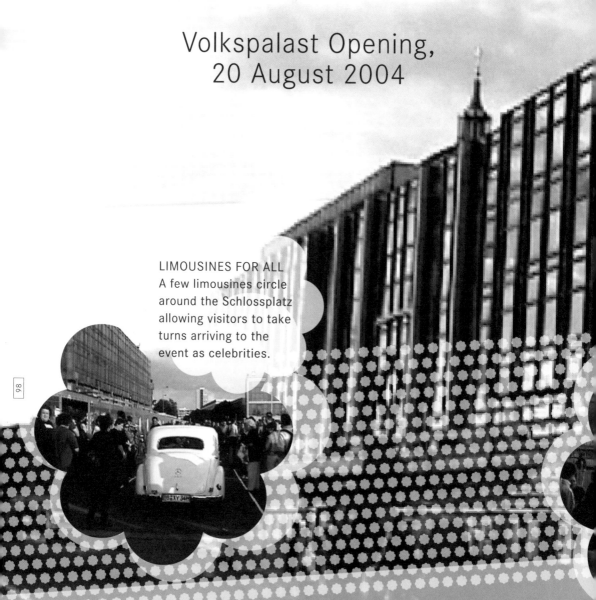

Volkspalast Opening,
20 August 2004

LIMOUSINES FOR ALL
A few limousines circle
around the Schlossplatz
allowing visitors to take
turns arriving to the
event as celebrities.

THE "VOLKSPALAST" (PEOPLE'S PALACE) PROJECT   Having been pushed to the forefront by
the process of unification, Berlin now runs the risk of becoming a bastion of defence: its
conquests and former momentum have faded and it is now fighting on the back foot. Faced
with such a lack of drive, a new experiment is being developed in the heart of the city: the
"Palace of the Republic", a gift from the past waiting to be granted a new use. This bare
skeleton, which currently permeates only emptiness, represents a unique space; a space
that highlights the tension between the past and the future, a space of transition.
Thanks to this "open" dimension, the 'Palace' shows great potential quite unlike any other
location in the Republic, in that it can be transformed into a provisional cultural centre
used to host experimental projects that will be highly attractive to the international
community. The temporary use of this place, which is full of references to the past and
symbolism, will provide new ways to explore the unknown. http://www.volkspalast.com/_vp/splashf.htm

GRAND OPENING The red carpet leads to a red ribbon that is repeatedly cut, restrung, and cut again, in a reception ceremony by every new group of visitors.

EVENTS   Since its opening, a wide variety of cultural events such as the recent Fun Palace Berlin 200X conference: http: //www.volkspalast.com/ _vp/a15.htm, an architectural debate disucussing the future of the Palast der Republik, have taken place in the Volkspalast.

© Photography: David Baltzer
(pages 100-103)

Bonn > Oliver Heissner

From the series *Empty Rooms* (2004)

Fifteen years after the fall of the Berlin Wall and five years after the German government moved from Bonn to Berlin, most places that once acted as the backdrop for the historical development of the Federal Republic now display emptiness and await an uncertain future. The first Chancellor of Germany, Konrad Adenauer, also held the position of President of the Koenig Museum. This building, which originally housed a zoological museum, was selected as the new seat for the government, as it was the only suitable property that had remained undamaged after the bombings of the Second World War. As was done in the past, numerous stuffed animals are once again on display in artificial surroundings.

It was in the Hall of the Federal Council, which displayed the typical neutral décor of the fifties, that the first constitution of the Federal Republic of Germany was proclaimed. The official invited guests of the Chancellor were received in Schaumburg Palace. The halls of the Federal Press Conference and the Press Club (meeting points for government members and those in charge of the media, acting as public representatives) also failed to inspire any true feelings of authority or power. Quite the opposite in fact, for they conveyed an atmosphere of neutrality, comparable to those of sports halls or spas. The so-called "World Hall" of the Ministry of External Affairs was where politicians met and made decisions with far-reaching consequences. Its sole decoration was a modestly sized world map that served as a symbol of how the small country of Germany had become part of the international community.

Bonn's "Hotel am Petersberg" not only welcomed "important public representatives", politicians and guests of the State, but is also the site where the first treaty with Allied forces was signed. The conference on Afghanistan was also held in the hotel.

The photographs on display are not aimed at merely documenting these important locations, which were the home to major political activity, but also hope to take a detailed and artistic look at the places that were originally overflowing with history but now have been stripped of their former significance. These places, which were once host to the political world, now lack even the human presence. They are a political stage without any appearance from the actors themselves.

Before long, these artistic works will form part of a complex exhibition, which will boast the collaboration of stage designer Lars Peter. A catalogue accompanying the exhibition is also to be published.

Foreign Affairs Office, Hall of the World

Schaumburg Palace

Museum König, Grand Hall

Press Club

Senate (Hall of the Federal Council)

Press conference room

Hotel Petersberg

112

→ **VERB**

In the face of a non-typical situation: the redevelopment of an entire city centre.
This type of redevelopment is possible in Almere due to it relative youth, less than
twenty years old. OMA submitted the award-winning competition entry and details
of Almere's new master plan are documented in this section.

Almere, 25 Km East of Amsterdam

Stadshart ● Almere

Master plan for urban redevelopment > Floris Alkemade, OMA

ALMERE IS NEXT TO AMSTERDAM, ON LAND RECLAIMED FOR A COMPLETELY NEW TOWN. COMPARED TO OTHER RESIDENTIAL AREAS IN THE REGION, POPULATION GROWTH STILL TAKES PLACE WITHIN THE URBAN AREA. IT WAS PLANNED IN THE 1970S, WHEN, IN URBAN PLANNING, URBAN QUALITIES WERE REGARDED AS SUSPECT, AND ATTEMPTS WERE MADE TO DISGUISE THIS NEW TOWN AS A COLLECTION OF VILLAGES.

DESPITE THAT INTENTION, ALMERE'S PROXIMITY TO AMSTERDAM LED TO ITS RAPID GROWTH; IN 1971 THERE WERE 47,000 INHABITANTS, TODAY IT HAS 170,000 AND IT IS EXPECTED TO EVENTUALLY GROW TO 450,000, MAKING IT HOLLAND'S FOURTH OR FIFTH CITY IN TERMS OF POPULATION.

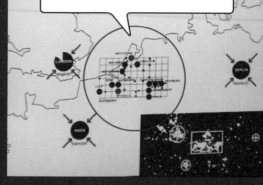

THE BRUSSELS-AMSTERDAM AREA CONSTITUTES A NEW METROPOLITAN SITUATION THAT IS NOT CONCENTRATED LIKE PARIS, LONDON OR BERLIN, BUT SPREAD OUT.

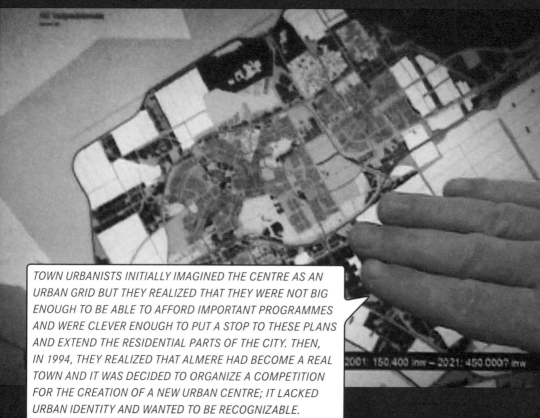

TOWN URBANISTS INITIALLY IMAGINED THE CENTRE AS AN URBAN GRID BUT THEY REALIZED THAT THEY WERE NOT BIG ENOUGH TO BE ABLE TO AFFORD IMPORTANT PROGRAMMES AND WERE CLEVER ENOUGH TO PUT A STOP TO THESE PLANS AND EXTEND THE RESIDENTIAL PARTS OF THE CITY. THEN, IN 1994, THEY REALIZED THAT ALMERE HAD BECOME A REAL TOWN AND IT WAS DECIDED TO ORGANIZE A COMPETITION FOR THE CREATION OF A NEW URBAN CENTRE; IT LACKED URBAN IDENTITY AND WANTED TO BE RECOGNIZABLE.

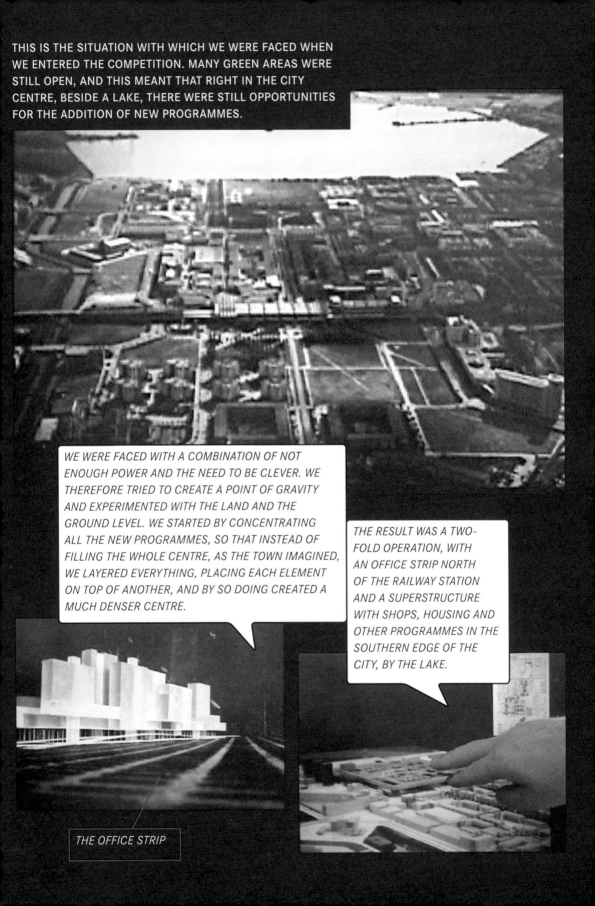

THIS IS THE SITUATION WITH WHICH WE WERE FACED WHEN WE ENTERED THE COMPETITION. MANY GREEN AREAS WERE STILL OPEN, AND THIS MEANT THAT RIGHT IN THE CITY CENTRE, BESIDE A LAKE, THERE WERE STILL OPPORTUNITIES FOR THE ADDITION OF NEW PROGRAMMES.

WE WERE FACED WITH A COMBINATION OF NOT ENOUGH POWER AND THE NEED TO BE CLEVER. WE THEREFORE TRIED TO CREATE A POINT OF GRAVITY AND EXPERIMENTED WITH THE LAND AND THE GROUND LEVEL. WE STARTED BY CONCENTRATING ALL THE NEW PROGRAMMES, SO THAT INSTEAD OF FILLING THE WHOLE CENTRE, AS THE TOWN IMAGINED, WE LAYERED EVERYTHING, PLACING EACH ELEMENT ON TOP OF ANOTHER, AND BY SO DOING CREATED A MUCH DENSER CENTRE.

THE RESULT WAS A TWO-FOLD OPERATION, WITH AN OFFICE STRIP NORTH OF THE RAILWAY STATION AND A SUPERSTRUCTURE WITH SHOPS, HOUSING AND OTHER PROGRAMMES IN THE SOUTHERN EDGE OF THE CITY, BY THE LAKE.

THE OFFICE STRIP

THE COUNCIL LIKED OUR PROPOSAL FOR AN OFFICE STRIP
AND THE WAY WE GAVE IT AN IDENTITY, BUT IN THE OTHER
DOWNTOWN THEY WERE WORRIED ABOUT THE CONTRASTING
SCALES BETWEEN OUR PROPOSAL AND THE EXISTING CITY,
AND THEREFORE ASKED US TO CUT UP OUR PLAN SO THAT IT
WOULD FIT INTO THEIR ORIGINAL GRID PLAN IDEA.

OUR RESPONSE WAS THAT SINCE
THE EXISTING URBAN PLAN WAS
BASED ON A SYSTEM OF DEAD-END
STREETS, SOME FOR PEDESTRIANS
AND SOME FOR BUSES, THIS WAS
NOT A GRID CITY BUT SOMETHING
ELSE. WE TRIED TO CONVINCE THEM
THAT IF WE SUPERIMPOSED ALL THE
ELEMENTS WE COULD INTRODUCE
NEW FREEDOM INTO THE PLAN.

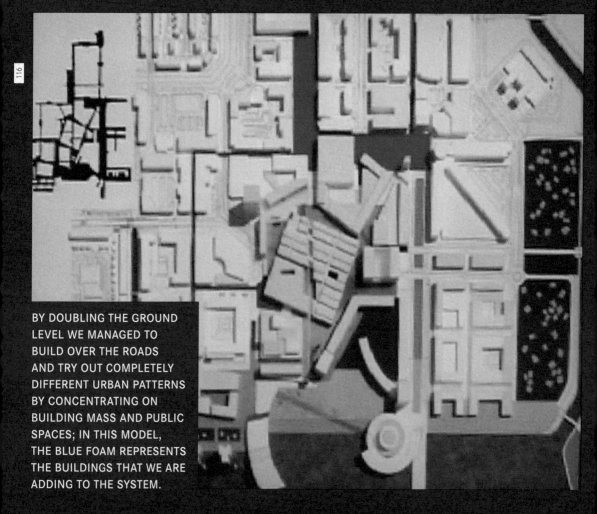

BY DOUBLING THE GROUND
LEVEL WE MANAGED TO
BUILD OVER THE ROADS
AND TRY OUT COMPLETELY
DIFFERENT URBAN PATTERNS
BY CONCENTRATING ON
BUILDING MASS AND PUBLIC
SPACES; IN THIS MODEL,
THE BLUE FOAM REPRESENTS
THE BUILDINGS THAT WE ARE
ADDING TO THE SYSTEM.

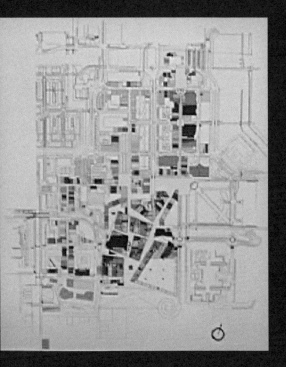

THE NEW SYSTEM SHOULD BE READ AS TWO CITIES PLACED ONE ON TOP OF THE OTHER: A LOWER LAYER WITH CAR PARKING BUT ALSO WITH ROADS, SHOPS AND SOME SQUARES, GARDENS OR PUBLIC SPACES, COVERED BY A CURVED DECK THAT ESTABLISHES A SEAMLESS CONNECTION WITH THE REST OF THE CITY. THIS DECK RISES TOWARDS THE CENTRE OF THE NEW DEVELOPMENT AND DESCENDS TOWARDS THE WATER, SO THAT THE LEVEL THERE IS THE SAME AS IN THE GARAGE BELOW THE CENTRAL PART OF THE DECK.

A CURVED DECK

THIS SLOPE PRODUCES A VERY GENEROUS SPACE IN THE CENTRE THAT IS SIX METRES HIGH AND MUCH MORE SPACIOUS THAN A NORMAL PARKING FLOOR.

NEXT TO THE PARKING SPACE WE HAVE PUBLIC PROGRAMMES SUCH AS SHOPS, A BOWLING ALLEY AND A FITNESS CENTRE. THE TWO LEVELS ARE REALLY MIXED, AND WE TRIED TO COMBINE THE BEST OF BOTH WORLDS WITHOUT CONDEMNING THE LOWER LAYER TO INFERIORITY.

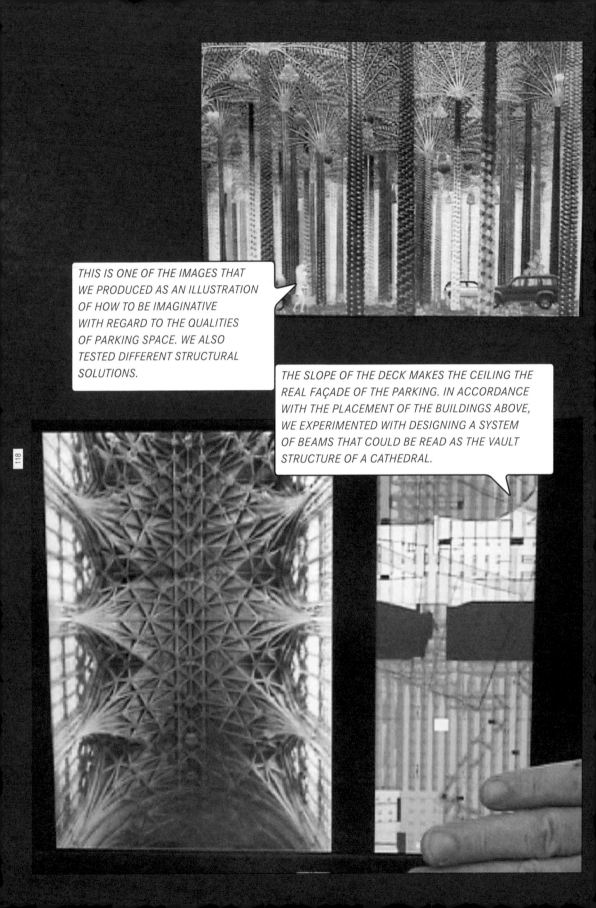

BLOCK 6

3.50 ~ +2.50 NAP - DECK LEVEL

CONSTRUCTION STARTED BY BUILDING OVER THE ROADS SO THAT THE
REST OF THE CONSTRUCTION SITE WOULD CONTINUE OVER THE TRAFFIC.
THE BUILDINGS HAVE BEEN ASSIGNED TO DIFFERENT ARCHITECTS:
WILLIAM ALSOP AND CLAUS EN KAAN HAVE ALREADY FINISHED THEIR
PROJECTS, CONSTRUCTION OF THE THEATRE BY SANAA HAS JUST STARTED
AND WE ARE COMPLETING A CINEMA COMPLEX.

Almere Urban Redevelopment > Office for Metropolitan Architecture

COMPETITION, 1994/1995, FIRST PRIZE   Almere, now over 100,000 inhabitants, has existed for less than two decades. In that short time the city has demonstrated enormous potential and vitality. It has shown a commitment to architectural innovation and experimentation. Almere will soon reach the critical mass that will enable it to redefine its ambitions; ten years from now, the population will approach that of an average medium-sized city. Then it will be possible to make the quantum leap from an agglomeration of distinct "equal" centers, each with its own concentration of facilities, to a city with a recognizable hierarchy in programmatic development. This growth will provide the city center with the basis for a number of essential facilities; such as a cultural nucleus (museum, library, theatre) and large scale retail facilities.

The center of Almere also offers the combination of easy accessibility by car and train, and the availability of building sites, both on the periphery as well as in the center. This means that a new urban office park can be developed in the center with accessibility and visibility equal to that of a peripheral location.

To mark the quantum leap in Almere, OMA decided to concentrate new program for the city and business center on only two sites: between the town hall square and the boulevard alongside the Weerwater and between the station and the planned Nelson Mandela Park. This concentration is essential for the unambiguous delineation of Almere's new status. It will also make it possible to create a new and recognizable form that contrasts with the existing, low density elements (specialist retailers, small-scale offices) which make Almere what it is today.

The chosen density necessitated the building of a 130,000m² office complex north of the station, taking maximum advantage of its location. The density of the shopping complex means that the boulevard can be freed from the planned commercial program, leaving space for cultural and leisure programs. This concentration also offers the opportunity to create a diagonal short-cut between the two shopping districts. The strip to the east of the center will be preserved from immediate development and offers an attractive location for a new expansion initiative later on.

COMMISSION, 1995   The next phase of the urban design is a cooperation of consultants from private development agencies, OMA, engineering consultants and a special agency from the City of Almere (project bureau). The OMA competition design has been further developed in this stage and has been tested for its functional and financial feasibility. Almere is a poly-nucleated agglomeration, where traffic and zoning are hierarchies in a Sixties-like fashion. Functional separation is maintained in the existing center as well, which in the form of a grid fakes a "traditional" city. Our proposal superimposes pedestrians and buildings onto a layer that organises all infrastructures, creating a density of public presence in the (new) center as a place "other," different than the existing city in terms of density, spatial diversity and orientation, achieving a place of maximum public interaction.

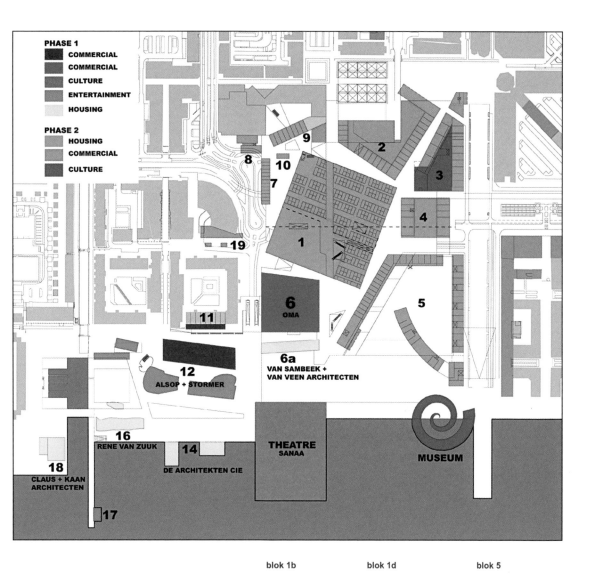

PHASE 1
- COMMERCIAL
- COMMERCIAL
- CULTURE
- ENTERTAINMENT
- HOUSING

PHASE 2
- HOUSING
- COMMERCIAL
- CULTURE

9

2

8

10

3

7

4

19

1

5

6
OMA

11

6a
VAN SAMBEEK +
VAN VEEN ARCHITECTEN

12
ALSOP + STORMER

16
RENE VAN ZUUK

14
DE ARCHITEKTEN CIE

THEATRE
SANAA

MUSEUM

18
CLAUS + KAAN
ARCHITECTEN

17

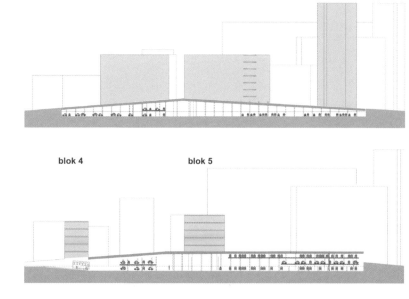

blok 1b   blok 1d   blok 5

blok 4   blok 5

MASTERPLAN   In this stage the private development agencies defined in detail the commercial programs for the center. The program mix is composed of approx. 53,000m^2 commercial, 9,000m^2 leisure, 1,100 housing units and 4,300 constructed parking spaces. The commercial concepts were tested on the proposed urban blocks and the hybrid combination of programs. The boulevard alongside the Weerwater is utilised for leisure, nightlife and cultural programs in order to achieve a vital waterfront.

The office complex has been developed in further detail. Similar to the City Center, a sloping plane (covering a carpark) provides pedestrian access to the office buildings. The plinth of each building consists of service programs (copy centers, conference rooms, employment agencies, shops, etc.), which are complementary to the offices above. Towers are tightly place, allowing horizontal connections through "bridges". This configuration allows larger buildings to be composed of smaller and – for corporate identity – district units. Construction of the first building began in December 1998.

MASTERPLAN URBAN REDEVELOPMENT, ALMERE. THE NETHERLANDS   www.oma.nl

Project: Almere, Masterplan Urban Redevelopment. Status: Competition 1998. Completion 2005. Client: City of Almere. Budget: 1.2B €. Location: Almere, Netherlands. Site: Centre of new town on regained land. Program: 1000 housing units; retail 53,000m^2; 4,300 constructed parking spaces; leisure 9,000m^2; theatre 8,000m^2; concert hall 2,000m^2; library 8,000m^2; arts school 7,000m^2; extension hospital with 32,000m^2 and 600 parking spaces; offices 130,000m^2; extension Almere Central Station, hotel 100 rooms, waterfront of 1km and infrastructure. Principal: Rem Koolhaas. Project Director: Floris Alkemade. Project Architect: Rob de Maat. Team: Olga Aleksakova, Bina Bhatta-charya, Bart Cardinaal, Kees van Casteren, Markus Detteling, Philip Koenen, Karen Shanski, Shohei Shiglatsu, Mark Watanabe.

Wouter Vanstiphout:*

"Almere is an example of 1960s typology; a gigantic megastructure with architecture stuck on it. I like Almere because it embraces the consumer culture that you see everywhere. It is the ultimate consumer city, and I think that OMA's project responded to that very well. It looks like avant-garde architecture, but it could have been anything else. MAB, the construction company, did another inner-city development in The Hague at the same time, and there they worked with Rob Krier as the masterplan architect. This shows how interchangeable the design is to the developer – Almere has always branded itself as a happy progressive place, with modern architecture, and so for them it made sense to choose Koolhaas, but in The Hague, which is the chic nineteenth century administrative center, they decided to take a neo-nineteenth century architect. OMA is literally doing urban design there, design on the scale of a whole city."

* See *WIMBY!* on page 128

Blok 6 > OMA

In the overall master plan for Almere, Blok 6 sits between the entertainment-oriented waterfront and the built-up shopping centre. Together with the facing, wedge-shaped apartment block of equal height (Blok 6A, developed by van Sambeek & van Veen), Block 6 forms a larger whole. On the pedestrian level and in the garage, it is surrounded by passages that connect the different parts of the new city centre. The garage slips under

the building, reducing its footprint on this level. The building meets three different entrance levels: the garage, the city street level in the northwest corner of the building and the deck level with entrances on three sides. Due to the slope of the pedestrian deck (the *gebogen maaiveld*), the connections to the deck have a height difference with a maximum of 2.10 metres.

How does one design a building based on a programme assembled for its economic potential rather than its building type? How does one create an identity that is not based on an architectural typology? How does one deal with the diverse interests and ruthless rate of change inherent in a commercial programme? How does one conceptualize a building for a site which is vacant, yet already planned to a high degree of specificity? Rather than being conceptualized typologically, the identity of this building (its 'added value') was derived from its organization. A generic volume, accommodating a commercial programme, was divided into mass and void – where mass contains the programme outside the architect's control and void is a volume in which a more coherent identity can be orchestrated. The lower mass houses shops that follow the requirements of their own identities, be it brand or product-based. The stores are continuously re-created by interior architects,

shop-window designers, decorators and marketing people. The upper mass contains the closed volumes of the cinema and projection spaces that change their content even more rapidly. The void employs the synergy of the different programmes to create a new identity, determining the overall character of the block and defining its attraction. This space allows for all connections between the pedestrian level and the cinema auditoriums. It has been organized in such a way that all circulation is located on top of the shopping mass. The void fulfils its obligations without any additional floors or balconies, maximizing its spatial presence. The spatial continuity of the void from the top balcony, to the pedestrian level and down to the garage, exposes its activity to the square. The shops and the restaurant even out the irregular activity of the cinema with its peaks of congestion and hours of invisible activity.

Since the void is created though the absence of mass, identity is determined by the void's surface. With the flexibility of graphic information, the surface can cope with the rapid obsolescence of shopping environments – "info-babble" as wallpaper.

In collaboration with ABT, the basics of the construction were defined.

Since the walls of the elevated auditoriums are made of half-sized, lattice-steel girders it was possible to cantilever all of the auditoriums by connecting them though a central structural zone. This zone supports the entire load of the upper part of the building. Consequently, the void space is cleared of any visible structure and achieves maximum flexibility and spatial clarity. In collaboration with the Adviesburo van Hooft, it was decided to fit the building with sprinklers. This choice has several advantages: it removes the need for fire compartments, thereby maintaining the openness and flexibility of the building; the steel structure of the cinema requires less fire protection and the exit stairs can be downsized and set back from the façade.

BLOK 6, ALMERE. THE NETHERLANDS   www.oma.nl

Project: Blok 6. Status: Commission 1998. Client: MAB. Budget: 22.6M €. Location: Almere, The Netherlands. Site: In the future City Centre on top of large scale parking garage. Program: 19,135m²: cinema 7,680m², 10 auditoria, 2,028 seats, 3.3m² per seat, lobby 1,615m²; commercial & mega store 3,260m², small retails 1,100m², restaurant 1,280m², supermarket 3,230m², loading dock 1,120m²; storage 585m². Principal: Rem Koolhaas. Project Director: Floris Alkemade. Team: Olga Aleksakova, Bina Bhattacharya, Bart Cardinaal, Kees van Casteren, Rob de Maat, Laszlo Fecske, Sharon Goren, Philip Koenen, Antti Lassila, Paz Martin, Markus Schaefer, Karen Shanski, Shohei Shiglatsu, Mark Watanabe with Christina Beaumont, Tobias Reinhardt, Lutz Ring.

→ VERB

The Netherlands: The following pages describe the reality of Hoogvliet, an old town near Rotterdam which has suffered much decay and neglect in the last thirty years. In order initiate revitalize it, WiMBY! was created and the architects Michelle Provoost and Wouter Vanstiphout elected to define the program. This is their story.

Conversation with Wouter Vanstiphout

"Hoogvliet is part of the municipality of Rotterdam, and although it is separated from it, what goes on here is a product of what goes on in the city, especially in South Rotterdam, where all the harbors are emptying out. That's the most problematic part of Rotterdam, with some neighborhoods where 80-90% of the population is immigrant, and also where the list of Pim Fortuyn received 70% of the votes in the last elections to the parliament. Pim Fortuyn himself lived in South Rotterdam, in the same urban bleakness that his party benefitted from."

Hoogvliet, Rotterdam, 2004

WiMBY!

Welcome Into My Back Yard! International Building Exhibition
Michelle Provoost / Wouter Vanstiphout

Happy Hoogvliet > Michelle Provoost

Only six kilometers long, Rotterdam's subway line was the shortest in the world when it opened in 1968. Not surprisingly, the city took great pride in having built the Netherlands' first subway. It was yet another sign of the city's agility in re-inventing itself after the devastating air raid that had destroyed its historical core in 1940. It manifested the two pillars of Rotterdam's carefully cultivated image: modernity and progress. A new urban core dominated by buildings that meant business (to quote Richard Yates' Revolutionary Road), and spacious new housing estates fostered the city's self-esteem. The subway was welcomed as a gadget that strengthened the new image. Starting in the rebuilt center, the line crosses the river, revealing the old working class estates on the southern bank. It continues to the postwar housing estates that endlessly repeated series of identical or very similar units (which had appropriately been labeled 'stamps'). For the time being the line ended in Slinge station, in one of the world's most famous housing estates: Pendrecht. The first designs for Pendrecht had been made by a vanguard of modern architects from the CIAM: Van den Broek & Bakema and Lotte Stam-Beese. The purity of the design and the much famed spatial concept had transformed it into a model that inspired similar experiments all over Europe. It was one of the highlights of Dutch urban planning. The line was soon extended beyond the city's municipal borders. First it reached the stations in Rhoon and Poortugaal. Here, even though we have barely left Rotterdam behind us, the city seems light-years away. Small villages accentuate the dikes, there are small shops, churches and quite a number of farms: a typical Dutch countryside. Green pastures show up on both sides of the subway line, willows mark the course of narrow country roads, sheep graze the banks. Then suddenly, one of the new housing estates appears and we feel back in Rotterdam. Station Hoogvliet is lined with high-rise blocks and large apartment buildings. It is the city's farthest outpost, 12 kilometers away from the center. Hoogvliet is a veritable New Town, an autonomous urban unit designed in the late 1940s according to the principles of the English New Towns near London.

The reason to build Hoogvliet this far from the existing city was the passionate desire to do more than only repair the destruction caused by the war: the port of Rotterdam was to become the largest in the world. To achieve this ambitious goal, in the Botlek and Europoort areas, huge new harbor basins were created and complemented by new industrial complexes. The small medieval village of Hoogvliet, situated in the immediate vicinity of the Shell refinery, was singled out as a 'nucleus of growth', suitable for housing the labor

"The church is the only remaining building on this side of the road of the old village that existed here before, and there are a few other remaining old buildings on the other side.... This has become the iconic image of our project – a temporary square partly used as a parking lot with a forgotten church next to it."

force needed by the expanding port. Gradually, the old village was to be replaced by a completely new Hoogvliet. The historical port was filled in, historical farms and characteristic small houses along the dikes were demolished. As a prelude to these grand ideas, the old core near the seventeenth-century church (that escaped demolition) was destroyed to make place for the New Town's shopping center. The scale of this shopping mall was quite large: the plan envisaged shops, high-rise apartment buildings, cultural buildings including a musical center, and a sports stadium. Hoogvliet was to become a regional center, a sparkling magnet attracting people from the neighboring villages. Lotte Stam Beese's drawings of Hoogvliet radiate a practical, urbane atmosphere comparable to Harlow or Stevenage, quite different from the famous housing estate Pendrecht. Hoogvliet was to be a proud and independent urban core next to Rotterdam.

SUCCESSES AND FAILURES

In its urban lay-out, Hoogvliet clearly reflected the ideals of the neighborhood unit. The social hierarchy of family, neighbors, the neighborhood community and the urban society was mirrored by the physical hierarchy of the individual house, the street, a group of streets with a small shopping center, the neighborhood and the city at large. All housing units were designed as parts of a balanced community composed of various types of houses. The architecture of the houses, schools, and shops was sober and homogenous. This functionalist feeling was greatly enhanced by the industrial building methods that were applied in Hoogvliet. Apart from that, the town expressed one of the great ideals of the time: social equality. An abundance of open spaces and collective gardens compensated for the small houses; the transparency and openness of the public greenery represented a new, open urban society. Naturally, traffic was organized according to the latest ideas on efficiency. Cars, bicycles and pedestrians were provided with their own special lanes. These were combined to create wide traffic arteries provided with ample greenery: a modern version of the American parkway. All components of the urban structure were endowed with the qualities of modernism and efficiency, simultaneously manifesting an idealistic social model. Like most post-war utopias, the ideal New Town of Hoogvliet soon experienced serious difficulties. Instead of fostering social cohesion, the neighborhood units promoted a feeling of contingency. In nearby Vlaardingen, sociologists discovered that inhabitants identified with their street and its immediate surroundings, but not with the social module of the neighborhood. To add insult to injury, the size of the houses was considered too small. Lacking an extra room that might be used as a study, the houses offered in Hoogvliet were bound to have a devastating effect on the development of the individual personality, at the

same time hampering opportunities to have a harmonious family life. This was all the more serious because the population of Hoogvliet was made up of a curious mix of immigrants from the agrarian provinces of Drenthe and Zeeland. They had their own dialect, clung to their own lifestyles and formed a source of continuous friction. Finally, the possibility to transform Hoogvliet into an autonomous New Town was questionable right from the start. Rotterdam was nearby, and after the construction of the subway line and new highways in the 1960s, the inhabitants of Hoogvliet were no longer dependent on the amenities offered in Hoogvliet. What had been conceived as one of the blessings of Hoogvliet, its situation at a stone's throw from the Shell refinery, turned out to be a major setback, due to a series of accidents and the continuously polluted atmosphere. On January 20, 1968, an explosion shattered most of the windows in Hoogvliet, dramatically changing its image from a friendly, efficient and modern city into the stigma of a place that could better be avoided.

Even before Hoogvliet lost its utopian aura, town planners had understood that its location was far from ideal. In the beginning of the 1960s, when new housing estates where still being added and the population of the New Town grew rapidly, the planners decided that the original vision of a city inhabited by some 60.000 people had become problematic. They decided to extend the subway line, adding one more stop to create Spijkenisse, at a safe distance from the industrial complexes. Spijkenisse was to develop into a New Town of approximately 80.000 people. The housing estates originally intended to be part of Hoogvliet were transferred to Spijkenisse. With it, the image of an optimistic, desirable housing estate definitely left Hoogvliet. Hoogvliet never had more than 37.000 inhabitants. Of the ambitious plans for a shopping mall with numerous cultural and recreational facilities, only some shops remained. Decades later, rows of suburban one family houses were built on the area that was left open. Even today, the area near the church gives the impression of a suburban wasteland, only used for parking (see page 131). Instead of the urban, even semi-metropolitan character originally meant to single out Hoogvliet's housing estates, the last parts that were built show a typically suburban character, defined by small, meandering streets lined with single family houses. Lost within one of these estates, stuck between

"Hoogvliet and Rotterdam: Hoogvliet is limited on one side by much more prosperous suburbs and little towns that do not belong to the municipality of Rotterdam but that lie all around it, and by the Shell refinery on the other. Hoogvliet doesn't look like Rotterdam, but it represents the same large urban dilemmas that you don't have in the suburbs. People in Hoogvliet feel an inferiority complex to the much richer communities around them, and also a kind of rebelliousness towards Rotterdam, because they feel that they would be better off if they were independent, and that they would be able to become competitive with these surrounding suburbs."

the remnants of old dikes, the subway station is a far cry from the direct access to the very urban center that was originally planned. The entry to the city is marked by a vast and desolate square used as a bus station, where ten surrealistically shaped bus stops all await the same line: no. 78. Whoever enters Hoogvliet at this point cannot help but remember the feelings of the town planners in the late 1960s: Hoogvliet is a town planning accident. It has become a mutant: half New Town, half suburb.

GHETTO

It may be true that Hoogvliet failed to live up to its promises of a New Town, and it is hard to deny that the dream of the modernist city became discredited here even before half of the project had been realized. Even so, Hoogvliet does exist and is here to stay. In the mid-1990s, over 30.000 people lived here, some of them the middle-aged 'pioneers' of the 1950s and 1960s. They liked Hoogvliet because for them it was a quiet place at a comfortable distance from the increasingly problem-ridden metropolis of Rotterdam. Many of the former inhabitants of Hoogvliet – those who could afford to move – had left the tiny, noisy homes and settled in the bigger houses of the surrounding cities. The inexpensive houses of Hoogvliet attracted new inhabitants: Hoogvliet became a refuge for immigrants, many of them from the Netherlands Antilles. They took up residence in the northern parts of Hoogvliet, where their different lifestyles soon caused trouble. It did not take long for a real schism to develop between the suburban, fairly well-to-do southern areas, which were mainly inhabited by native Dutch people, and the northern parts that were increasingly dominated by socially weaker groups. 'Nieuw Engeland', the 'oil'-estate, epitomized this new trend. In 1951, so-called fan-shaped flats had been erected there, lining streets named after regions rich in oil: Caracas street, Texas street. The homes in this area were especially small, built in somber brick and located at the least desirable part of Hoogvliet: close to the oil refinery alongside the highway. In the 1990s, these streets changed into what soon became known as a ghetto. Junkies, drugs dealers, and vandalism made Nieuw England an ideal topic for a Dutch television documentary that further strengthened the image of Hoogvliet as a sad and lost neighborhood.

REVITALIZING HOOGVLIET

To stop the downward trend, Hoogvliet proclaimed itself a disaster area in the mid-1990s. First of all, the fan-shaped flats were raided by the combined forces of the police, the public health service, tax collectors and bailiffs who combed all the apartments in an attempt to stop all illegal activities. Drugs dealers were imprisoned, defaulters indicted, illegal ten-

ants evicted. Subsequently, the remaining inhabitants were offered better houses elsewhere in Hoogvliet. The flats were demolished. Thus, the most disgraceful part of Hoogvliet had been dealt with in a heavy-handed manner, meant to set an example for the next projects. The local authorities and the two housing corporations that had recently been privatized and who owned most of the housing stock in Hoogvliet, cooperated in an attempt to improve housing conditions. No less than 5000 houses, 30% of the housing stock, were scheduled to be demolished, mainly flats of 56 square meters or smaller that could no longer live up to the expectations of the population of the 1990s. Likewise, the maisonette flats and the homes for the elderly, which had been built in the 1960s around small courtyards, all of them miniature houses with one small living room and an even smaller bedroom, were singled out for demolition. Marketable homes were to replace them. By creating a more diverse palette of housing types, reducing the rate of subsidized tenement housing (which used to be 70%), a more diverse and well-to-do population was expected to be willing to move to Hoogvliet.

The revitalization campaign for Hoogvliet was clearly an answer to concrete needs, but it also reflected fundamental changes in the Dutch Welfare State. The state withdrew from public life, a concept that led Public Housing to become almost completely privatized. The Housing Corporations shook off their traditional role as social organizations and started to be run as semi-commercial companies. This is the case, not only in Hoogvliet, but in almost all post-war housing estates that have undergone the processes of revitalization, leading to strategies that are determined more by administrative and commercial concerns than by social ideas. As Jaqueline Tellinga put it in a recent publication on 'The Big Reconstruction': 'Since their privatization in 1995, the corporations have turned into real estate companies in which decisions on investments are made at the highest level. They evaluate their possessions as part of their complete holdings, irrespective of their specific setting.'[1] For this reason they choose a generic approach for all reconstruction projects, in spite of how different the original situation may be. Everywhere, high-rise buildings and flats are substituted for low-rise, mostly single-family homes; private gardens replace collective greenery, small neighborhood shopping centers disappear, and large central shopping malls are designed in their place. Last but not least: low-cost tenement houses are suppressed and expensive owner-occupied houses strongly promoted.

The revitalization of Hoogvliet followed similar lines. To correct the negative image, most of the urban structure, the public spaces and housing stock, was to be replaced by something with a more 'contemporary' outlook. The characteristic composition of elementary blocks floating in space, so typical for the modern city, were considered out of date. They were replaced by enclosed spaces and traditional urban motives: the inner city street, the return of the building line as the main organizational principle, the square, the boulevard. The original concept of an introverted pedestrian shopping mall was turned inside-out by moving the shops to

"They demolish the high-rises because they contain most of the problems, and they replace them with low-rise apartments or even suburban-type houses so that they get better tax revenues, but then the people who lived in the high-rise buildings are scattered and pop up in other neighborhoods."

"This is our Hoogvliet office, one of the few remaining traces of the old Hoogvliet, before the modern planning started. It used to be a station for a train line to Rotterdam that no longer exists. ...When we came to work in Hoogvliet the old station master and his wife still lived here. But then the wife died and he went to a home, and the building was about to be demolished. We talked to the city in order to convince them to buy it and we found out that they already owned it, so we were allowed to rent it for free as long as we took care of the repairs and the renovation."

1. Jacqueline Tellinga, 'Corporaties zijn sinds hun verzelfstandiging in 1995 vastgoedmaatschappijen geworden waarbij de investeringsbeslissingen op hoog niveau in de organisatie worden genomeen. Ze beoordelen hun bezit vanuit hun complete vastgoedportefeuille, niet op buurt-niveau.', in J. Tellinga, *De Grote Verbouwing. Verandering van naoorlogse woonwijken*, Rotterdam 2004, p.20.

the boulevard. The free flowing public space that washed through Hoogvliet's urban tissue was to be framed by new blocks of houses, streets and cozy courtyards. Collective spaces, a fundamental principle of post-war town planning, had to make way for private gardens. Everything reminiscent of the original 'collective' ideals was banned. From then on, the individual and his personal lifestyle were to determine Hoogvliet.

In short, the most characteristic feature of the revitalization scheme was the urge to eradicate the modern model on which the original plan for Hoogvliet had been based. Everything associated with it was viewed negatively. The town planners' main aspiration was to reinvent Hoogvliet. Though they returned to tested traditional models, the planners' ambition to bulldoze most of the existing New Town is reminiscent of the tabula rasa mentality of their colleagues who first built Hoogvliet in the 1950s. The new plan did not relate to the existing situation any better than the original concept had related to the historical village it wanted to replace.

WIMBY!

In 1999, the alderman for physical planning, at the time a representative of Holland's Green Party, proposed a motion that urged for an International Building Exhibition modeled on the German example of the Internatione Bau Ausstellung (IBA) in Berlin and Emscher Park. It was a brave attempt to counter the prevailing currents in urban politics and the town planning profession, which were entirely focused on spectacular and highly prestigious projects in Rotterdam's inner city. Instead, the party wanted to direct attention to the slum-like conditions found in many of the post-war housing estates. The motion proved to be the starting point for the WiMBY! manifestation: Welcome in My Backyard. Since 2000, the management team has been led by Felix Rottenberg, former president of the Dutch Social-Democrat Party. The contents of the manifestation are defined by two architectural historians of Crimson, Michelle Provoost, author of this article, and Wouter Vanstiphout.

Even though the famous German projects inspired WiMBY!, it soon became clear that neither Berlin nor Emscher Park could provide a model for Hoogvliet. Not only was WiMBY! never more than a miniature version of these projects, its context was also very different. Whereas the Emscher Park project worked in a virtual vacuum – both the industries and the population tended to move away from the Ruhr region – Hoogvliet was bombarded with reconstruction proposals. There was more than enough funding and revitalization had already begun. The local political board, housing corporations and commercial realtors were engaged in what they termed the 'Hoogvliet conspiracy'. A conspiracy that promised to be very successful.

Then came WiMBY! What could WiMBY! possibly add to a planning machinery that was already in full swing? It's special assignment was to improve the quality of the revitalization scheme, to introduce innovative concepts on various levels: social, economic, architectural, urban, and – most importantly – to make their proposals actually happen. Visits to Emscher Park had helped to give the participants some clues as to what was to be expected: industrial ruins turned into cultural attractions, the promotion of high tech industries that built striking, modern offices, beautifully designed public spaces and magnificent light projects that attracted car loads of tourists from all over Europe. However – was this really what Hoogvliet needed? What kind of projects were possible, feasible, and necessary here?

It soon became clear that it was useless to create another separate organization, a true WiMBY! institute, to join the already existing organizations – this would only have led to time-consuming, competitive strife. Instead, we decided to concentrate on the existing planning machinery's blind spots. We decided to cause a coordinated series of incidents that should have a marked effect on Hoogvliet. First and foremost, the projects that we embarked upon would have a direct bearing to Hoogvliet and set an example for similar projects elsewhere.

Apart from engaging in concrete projects, we also wanted to change the public's mentality. Our focal point was the existing substance of Hoogvliet, both physical (the buildings) and social (the people). As in so many reconstructed housing estates, there was hardly time to reflect upon the object of so much planning fervor: the New Town of Hoogvliet. Nor had the results of research by sociologists, traffic experts, and town planning historians been properly assessed. WiMBY! identified the need to correct these shortcomings as a prerequisite for reinterpreting the worn out New Town. It wanted to rediscover its now hidden qualities as an unknown, captivating new urban entity with its own peculiarities. Reinterpreting and reusing what was already present should become the guiding principle in the reconstruction process. As a consequence, some projects – Domain Hoogvliet, Hoogvliet inside out, and WiMBY! Week – were on the verge of becoming social community work. Sometimes initiatives that bore no direct relation to architecture were most effective in presenting alternative approaches to the sometimes overly ambitious, large-scale reconstruction projects. Temporary interventions, cultural reprogramming or a one-time event could help to rediscover the New Town's hidden but positive qualities and above all, bring to light unexpected urban potentialities, possibly inspiring future strategies. This potential is located both in the inhabitants and in the existing urban fabric. It is an unanswered question whether or not a program based upon suburban and costly houses can ever generate such vitality.

ANTI TABULA RASA

We were absolutely sure that if Hoogvliet was to become a new, vital and attractive city within ten years, nothing would be more counterproductive than to start from scratch. The tabula rasa mentality that wants to raze everything it encounters, from buildings to underground infrastructure, may have been useful in the postwar reconstruction era, but in this case it was totally useless. Using existing qualities helps

"The attitude of these housing corporations and these developers is that these cities do not fit the way we live anymore, and so they need to be replaced by something that does fit. Our position on the other hand, is that by doing that you are again making something that fits the way we live now but that probably you will have to demolish again in 20 years."

to prevent the New Town from becoming generic, something that could have developed everywhere, in a suburb near Leeuwarden as well as in Enschede or Amersfoort. While the planning machinery set in motion by the corporations continuing the preparation for the demolition of thousands of homes, postulating the values of the new, quiet suburban middle-class Hoogvliet that was be created in its place, WiMBY! worked on a totally different concept of Hoogvliet. Hoogvliet was to resemble itself and not try to emulate other cities. It should find ways to deal with its green, village-like character and the ethnic make-up of its inhabitants, and it should cherish those positive opportunities manifested from itself. This approach called for a thorough analysis of Hoogvliet, focusing not only on problems and difficulties, but on its positive aspects. By stressing the negative qualities, the large-scale reconstruction process that had been going on for some time ignored the positive characteristics. No one mentioned the profuse greenery, public gardens, which were only seen as wasteland waiting to be developed. No one drew attention to the potentialities of the large community of people from the Netherlands Antilles, the problems of recent years having only left room for negative feelings. Thus, many qualities that could have inspired the revitalization process were just simply discarded – an approach that seems inherent in Rotterdam's 'progressive' tradition.

"We have our small office downstairs and upstairs we made the only hotel room in the whole town, which we use to invite journalists, artists or politicians to live here for two or three days and do some research, meet local people, and then produce a proposal, an analysis, a lecture or a drawing, whatever it is that they do."

Our deviant views on Hoogvliet were first published in a book in 2000: *WiMBY! Welcome into My Backyard!* Its cover illustrated our intentions quite eloquently: Hoogvliet's historical church is shown adjacent to a vast expanse of Stelcon slabs, symbols of the failure of the New Town but at the same time manifesting their own peculiar beauty.[2] This beauty is enhanced by Hoogvliet's unfinished character and can be seen in many places: the dike, which had to make place for the subway line, but simply continues on the other side of it, farms that look out of place between the flats, geese and sheep grazing in a setting of 1950s architecture. The WiMBY! Strategy demonstrates precisely these qualities by exaggerating even their tiniest specimens and by idealizing what went wrong. This analysis had distinct therapeutic features because it showed the inhabitants just how unique their New Town really is. Thus, their ingrained inferiority complex was healed. We expected to promote a change of mentality that might help to stop the purely negative way of dealing with the existing situation. One of the first urban projects of WiMBY! seems to confirm that this strategy may prove successful.

2. *WiMBY! Welcome Into My Backyard*. Internationale Bouwtentoonstelling Rotterdam-Hoogvliet, Rotterdam 2000.

LOGIC

Believing that Hoogvliet has many positive qualities, we needed a different type of town planning document than the all encompassing master plan. What was needed was a set of instruments that could help to steer the processes already at work, directing and manipulating them into a coherent policy. What was needed most, was to create some logic in the often conflicting projects initiated by the many institutions working in Hoogvliet. This is how Logic, a town planning manual for Hoogvliet came into being. It was designed by the Rotterdam based architectural firm of Maxwan Architects and Planners. Time and again, Logic emphasized the need for a joint approach in the 'Hoogvliet project'. Logic stated that so long as a coherent vision was lacking, the revitalization campaigns could only result in a chaotic, unremarkable, generic city in which the most important characteristics of the New Town would be lost. Logic identified the qualities that should be seen as Hoogvliet's main characteristics. Four urban devices were believed to result in a consistent structure: the green buffer surrounding the New Town, guaranteeing a rural setting on all sides, the isolated situation of the neighborhood, endowing each of them with its own particular values, the green joints between the neighborhoods containing the New Town's infrastructure, and finally the overall green qualities of Hoogvliet, a result of the fully mature trees in the open spaces and collective gardens.

Logic presented clear choices: each of the four structuring elements were put to the test. Were they to be respected or could one do without them? These issues were addressed in the so-called Logic committee that was made up of representative of all parties involved:

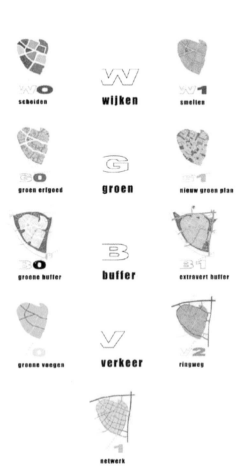

"With Maxwan we came up with this project where we brought together a number of people from these 5 decision-making groups and we started working on a kind of a game. We told them that Hoogvliet had 4 distinct spatial qualities: disappear, green, buffer, and highway... and you can either keep them or lose them. If you want to lose them, that is fine, but that should remain a centrally carried decision that could turn into a design agenda. If you want to keep them, that implies a very strategic design decision about the specific quality in question. ... We involved everyone in this whole "thinking appreciation" process. We then combined all these options and came up with 24 possible versions of Hoogvliet and described and named each one. Then, we valued the choices, from very possible to extremely difficult, only to be done with a huge central decision-making process involved, and presented this as the "Hoogvliet Logica Council.""

E I N D M O D E L

−"And which scheme is this?"

−"...this one." (01-W0G0B0GV)

"It is completely at one end of the spectrum. So the public wanted to keep everything the same, except for making the ring road. ...This is really a project that you can value only within 20 years."

01-W0G0B0V0

02-W0G0B0V1

03-W0G0B0V2

04-W0G0B1V0

05-W0G0B1V1

06-W0G0B1V2

07-W0G1B0V0

08-W0G1B0V1

09-W0G1B0V2

10-W0G1B1V0

11-W0G1B1V1

12-W0G1B1V2

13-W1G0B0V0

14-W1G0B0V1

15-W1G0B0V2

16-W1G0B1V0

17-W1G0B1V1

18-W1G0B1V2

19-W1G1B0V0

20-W1G1B0V1

21-W1G1B0V2

22-W1G1B1V0

23-W1G1B1V1

24-W1G1B1V2

CO-HOUSING SCHEME

"Co-Housing is a kind of re-invention of the Scandinavian commune. It is a group of people or families who come together and collectively approach a developer or architect who builds a mini, micro-neighborhood completely according to their wishes: what they want to share, what they don't want to share, what is the module for their houses, how to fill it in and which rules they want to set for each other.

It is a bit like a gated community, but more intimate and personal. One of the big questions for Hoogvliet was, "who would want to come live here?," and we turned this more into an autobiographical question: "What would Hoogvliet need to convince me to come and live here?"

Michelle worked on this, she has one child, and she asked herself what she would need to move. She thought, "of course Hoogvliet is boring, there is nothing to do here, none of my friends live here"...but the good thing of Hoogvliet is that there is so much space and, "if I could take up some of this space and live here with some of my friends, use nature and everything collectively, then it would be perfect."

The metro is very close by; you reach downtown Rotterdam in 15 minutes and be wonderfully close to nature, because the river is only 100m away.

Then we created this "Co-Housing" where a group of people who had a shared common interest, like growing organic cabbage, could come together, live together and then practice their interest collectively.

For example, this is how I currently live. Together with a few families, we bought an old school building, built it up and everyone customized their own part of the building and we share a main open space. A lot of times, everyone is sitting out in this space, and it is like a village within a village. A small niche group, of young, educated, and un-yuppie individuals, who are more culturally interested in trading one form of luxury for another, have become a significant group, in marketing terms.

This group of people live in the center of Rotterdam, have allotment gardens and are starting to have children. They want their children to have a garden but do not necessarily want to move into the suburbs. This Co-Housing project is interesting because it has become autobiographical, where basically I am trying to sell the image of Hoogvliet to myself."

DUPLEX FLATS: CLIP-ONS

"This whole area was supposed to be demolished, but an awful lot of money was spent renovating these flats about ten years ago. This makes it too expensive, financially, to demolish these flats now. So, after a lot of time of asking for some flats not to be demolished, we were given these flats to work with.

Somehow, a lot of the needier families of Hoogvliet happen to live in these flats. We had already been working with a group of single mothers, asking them what their ideal living environment would be. We went through a whole research process and thought that this opportunity, given to us by the housing corporation, for

extending the lives of these flats could be combined with the single mothers. We then asked a young firm from Rotterdam, named Krill, to do social research on these flats – research on a minute scale – which spaces were used for transit areas, which areas for meeting areas, very minute social research on how these families used the flats, about space inside the house,

immediately outside and around and which levels of intimacy does it have? It was a very precise anthropology of these spaces. Then Krill designed pragmatic tools to help address the problems of these flats instead of demolishing them.

Now they have designed very precise ways of changing the plans of the flats, as well as a "clip-on" element that would enlarge the galleries, which could be used as communal spaces and then would fit into a network of communal spaces and involve these existing central green spaces.

This flat will be the prototype and we have also asked for government subsidies. What we try to do in WiMBY is to really test things on the ground and build prototypes to test out solutions before implementation. For instance with the clip-ons, it is like having a whole second facade clipped onto the originally facade that creates all different types of new connections. These clip-ons help the flat to become more self-contained, while in fact they are also being networked. Also, some flats will be removed to create communal spaces with TVs or kitchens. We feel that people can have a perfectly comfortable life in these flats and it is not necessary to demolish them. And then, we show this through the prototypes."

the municipal planning board, the local political board, two corporations and the development agency of Rotterdam. The same issues were put before the residents on the WiMBY! website. Thus, Logic changed from a plan into a negotiation process. It yielded a binding choice for one of the 24 models that could be composed by combining the variables offered in the process. Remarkably, the strategy that was preferred opted for conserving and enhancing all existing qualities. Hoogvliet's green neighborhoods were to retain their self-contained qualities, flanked by wide parkways and surrounded by a recreational zone alongside the river Oude Maas.

NEW COLLECTIVES

While Logic addressed Hoogvliet's urban and physical qualities, other aspects of WiMBY! focused on its social qualities. Like the physical qualities, these were being grossly neglected, in spite of numerous the publicity campaigns and inquiry procedures organized by the official planning machinery. WiMBY! wanted more. We wanted to show what the inhabitants themselves had to offer. We wanted to exploit their creativity and make them responsible for projects we together with the residents. In doing so, we discovered that the concept of the collective was much more important than the official reconstruction campaign took it to be. Working with single mothers from the Antillean community, we found that they needed types of houses that combined the individual home with collective amenities and collective public spaces. The reconstruction campaign's implicit mantra: 'collective spaces have become impossible to maintain because the contemporary New Town lacks a collective mentality' may be true for the average Dutch family commuting from one place to the other in an ever expanding network city, but it does not apply to other groups. Judging from the growing number of communes, even among native Dutch, there appears to be a growing need for collective arrangements. These considerations fostered three projects we organized with the support of the housing corporations. They are intended to accommodate new collective housing arrangements. In one of the maisonettes – the most endangered type of house from the 1960s – a group of Antillean single mothers were provided with their own individual homes and a collective room that may be used as a crèche, a study or a café. Part of the surrounding public spaces will also be brought under collective control and designated as safe places for children to play and mothers to eat or party together. In another maisonette flat in the same part of Hoogvliet, homes for young people

"We presented the plans of an apartment complex that was still lived in, in colorful salons. The architectural propositions became lounging environments, cafes, cinemas and conversation pits. Architecture sneaked in, while the people of the apartment complex were given temporary facilities they never had before. We made a big, maybe even ham-fisted rhetorical statement, by turning 'Hoogvliet inside-out'. We projected enormous photos of the people of Hoogvliet and their spectacularly vernacular interiors on the bare facades. For some weeks the people and their aesthetic obsessions became the architecture of Hoogvliet, wiping away the bureaucratic expression of the modern architecture and making irrelevant the next generation of architectural order projected by the architects of the new Hoogvliet.

are planned that follow the so-called 'Foyer' model, which offers living, education and work. The third initiative attempts to attract categories of people have so far tried to avoid Hoogvliet. Even though Hoogvliet is easily accessible and has a lot to offer, its negative image rebuffs the more wealthy and creative layers of Rotterdam's population. How can we make Hoogvliet more attractive for these categories, that would add to the social diversity of Hoogvliet? The usual type of single family house with a garden can be found anywhere. As such, it cannot induce a move to Hoogvliet. It is conceivable that a type of co-housing might do the trick. Co-housing is a form of housing that combines twenty individual homes and a collective amenity that is assigned to them and managed by the twenty households living there. The nature of this collective entity is decided collectively. It can either be a crèche, an ecological garden, a car repair hall or a sports facility. Thus, a new meaning is given to the term 'collective housing'. The oppressive connotations associated with the collective arrangements of the 1950s are replaced by self-defined, contemporary forms that combine individual homes with a wide variety of opportunities to use public space.

COLLECTIVE SUBSTANCE
Judging from the way Hoogvliet manifests itself in its town planning an architecture, one would be inclined to think that its population must be homogenous. It is not. Behind the anonymous facades from the 1950s and 1960s, live a rich palette of people. They differ in income, ethnicity, and lifestyle and express these differences in the way they dress and the way they decorate their homes. The photo project 'Hoogvliet inside-out' asked dozens of people to have their pictures taken in a circulating photo tent: the elderly with their walkers, mothers with perms, hip hoppers acting tough, all kinds of people showed up. These portraits were complemented by interior photographs taken by Gerard Hadders and Edith Gruson. Subsequently, the portraits and the interior photos were blown up to larger than life billboards that were placed near the highway and at traffic signs in street crossings. Apart from that, they were used as propaganda for the WiMBY! week that was organized in December 2002 in a now demolished row of homes for the elderly. All WiMBY! projects were presented here, while half of the U-shaped row of houses remained occupied. The facades of the empty houses were used as huge billboards for the interior photos. All empty houses were dedicated to one of the WiMBY! projects, while historical movies were shown in the others. In one particular house, people could get their portraits taken while the elderly residents living nearby provided them with coffee. In this way, WiMBY! week not only show a diversity of WiMBY! projects, but also the wide variety of people living in Hoogvliet.

EDUCATION

What are the elements that make a city worth living in? The quality of the housing stock
and the shops, the facilities found there, the surroundings, the population, all these things
matter. In a depressed area, educational facilities are particularly important. Much needed
to be done to bring Hoogvliet's schools up to date. Most of
them had been built in the 1960s, many according to the standard types that were designed by the municipal authorities.
They are inconspicuous buildings in which the classrooms
are connected by long corridors. The special rooms needed
in present-day education are usually absent. It is difficult to
find a suitable place for teaching pupils on an individual basis,
for libraries, music performances, etc. The shabby concrete
buildings designed as temporary solutions when the schools
became overcrowded are hardly suitable for these purposes.
The need for special classrooms is further enhanced by the
changing make-up of Hoogvliet's population. More often than
not, children from various groups arrive at school without
having had breakfast. Provisions must be made to help the
parents. After school or during holidays, pupils have to be
taken care of. Improving the facilities for primary schools,
WiMBY! developed the so-called 'school parasites', which
were designed in cooperation with the Parasite Foundation.
For three schools, beautiful facilities were created where the
pupils can cook, eat, work by themselves or rehearse plays.

"We wanted to invent a
toolbox, or a box of tricks,
or a tune-up set, with which
modernly planned new towns
could be changed from within,
based on the dreams and
aspirations of the people
who live there or might want
to live there. This is a highly
paradoxical ambition; turning
anti-planning into a new
planning paradigm, turning
the local, highly specific
and undersigned into design
techniques that might work
as a global reference. We
swallowed our doubt and
moved on. Planning in a
modernist new town meant
opening up the design process
in the most drastic way."

The plans by Barend Koolhaas, Onix and Christoph Seyferth
can be industrially produced and are mobile. Apart from educational purposes, they can
also serve to accommodate neighborhood festivities, meetings and parent gatherings.
For secondary schools a special initiative was already on its way: the concentration of
three schools on a single campus. This allowed them to share sports facilities and the
auditorium. WiMBY! urged the participating parties to build this campus near the subway
station. This was seen as a remedy for the disadvantageous location of the subway station,
adding thousands of potential passengers, helping to make the station safer, and giving the
campus a function for the entire region. The campus is believed to make Hoogvliet a more
attractive place: nice houses can be found almost anywhere, a nice campus is something
special. Urging the schools in Hoogvliet to cooperate far more intensely than they were
accustomed to, we tried to improve Hoogvliet's educational system by promoting pupils to
move from one school to the other. This should reduce the terribly high dropout rate. The
subway station is presently framed by flats that are slated to be demolished and the campus will be integrated in the housing program, which is to replace them. This will result in
an ensemble of nice, small scale school buildings and collective facilities such as a library,
which can be used by both the pupils of the schools and the residents of the neighborhood.

SCHOOLPARASITES

a ruimte voor [Hoogvlietse] basisscholen

School Parasites -Provisional classrooms for primary schools - WiMBY! Rotterdam-Hoogvliet, Rotterdam, Valiz 2004.

Hoogvliet

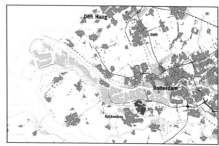

School Parasites project sites

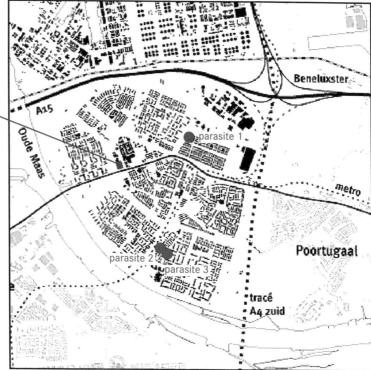

"The school parasites are strategic on a completely different level. What we did was to use the existing primary school buildings – which were just as uniformly produced as the whole area – to use them to focus completely on the program and as a metaphor of the design challenge of these postwar neighborhoods."

"As good architectural historians, we did a study of the history of these primary schools built in the 1950s, all belonging to a set of types based on modular systems: the block-school, the T-school, the H-school and the cross-school."

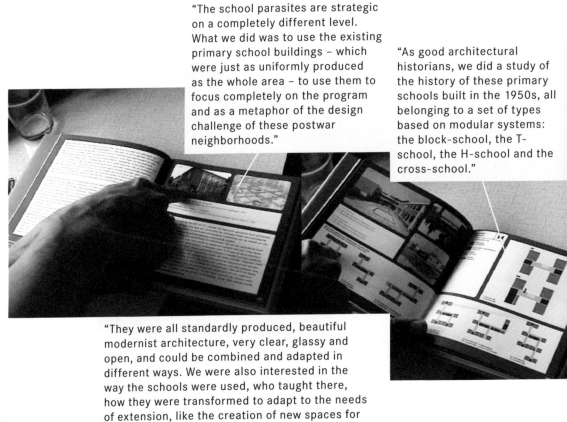

"They were all standardly produced, beautiful modernist architecture, very clear, glassy and open, and could be combined and adapted in different ways. We were also interested in the way the schools were used, who taught there, how they were transformed to adapt to the needs of extension, like the creation of new spaces for the computer. In a way there is a history of the architecture of these buildings by non-architects, of micro-architectural interventions."

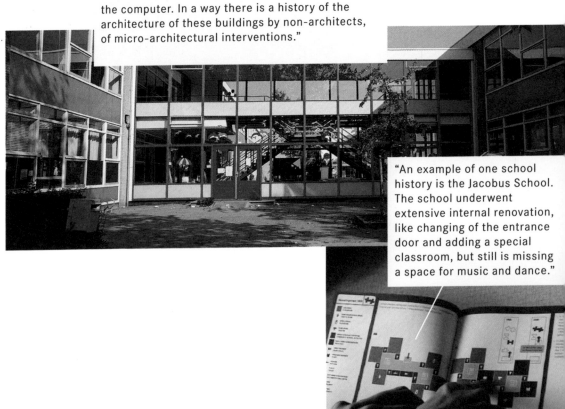

"An example of one school history is the Jacobus School. The school underwent extensive internal renovation, like changing of the entrance door and adding a special classroom, but still is missing a space for music and dance."

Need for new facilities like a computer room

Hoogvliet has a number of each type of these schools – you can find them in every Dutch post-war neighborhood. So you could say that there are thousands of areas like this in Holland, and they overlap in one set of problems, where the housing areas are no longer inhabited by the post-war, white, Dutch nuclear family, with more or less predictable everyday activities like taking children to school, going to the neighborhood shop everyday and to the city center in the weekends, etc. That doesn't work anymore.

"A lot of these schools are referred to now as "black schools" because most if not all of the pupils are non-European immigrants, who sometimes go to school without having had a proper breakfast. There is a high level of teenage pregnancy, they have nowhere to go in the afternoon, they have problems speaking Dutch which means that they need extra help for many things, some classes are overcrowded... In this new situation, the tasks of these old school buildings have grown exponentially, from serving breakfasts to teaching parents after the school's regular hours."

More than 70 % of the student population is of immigrant origin

Video comment: "Until now, they have rented pre-fabricated ugly containers to manage their problems, so the parasite project had to be realized in the same price but in better quality."

School Parasite 1 : Lampion (Chines lantern) > Designed by Christoph Seyferth

EATING & COOKING The schools need a space in which children can eat and cook. It should be a classroom with the atmosphere and intimacy of a living room. All activities that take place in a normal classroom can also be carried out here, but the environment will make lessons into a unique experience.

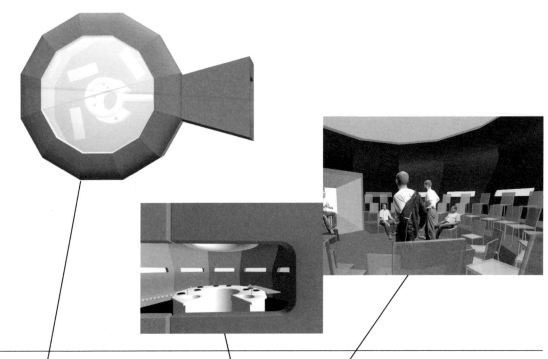

Christoph Seyferth designed a pavilion as a living room and meeting place. From the outside it is a mysterious object: a great Chinese lantern with a bench running round the exterior upon which you can have a sheltered seat, as though under a giant tree in an African village. Inside it is a festive, high space, sheltered like a living room, where you can eat and cook, but which is also suitable for innumerable other purposes: library, technology class, crafts and drawing, dramatic expression, performances, etc. The Chinese lantern offers children an experience of beauty that they, Seyferth hopes, will still remember vividly many years on. Inside, they can escape from the hectic - and for some children, boring school day, where hundreds of students are heaped into one building.
All facilities, including the kitchen, are located in the passageway connecting the Chinese lantern and the school. As desired, toilets or storage areas may also be included. The Chinese lantern can be used separately from the school building, for example to be used in neighborhood activities or to be rented to third parties.

Construction process: steel frames covered by polyesthel sheet.
The parasites' are 50 m² in area, equivalent to the size of a standard classroom.

"This is the kitchen unit. It is very important to teach to eat well, not only for the children but also for their parents, who are sometimes too young to know how to give their children breakfast. The shape of this building is like a sweet, a pretty piece of cake."

School Parasite 2 : Beest (Beast) > Designed by Onix

MUSIC The schools need a classroom for music and dance lessons, one which is also suitable for performances. It must be very quiet, but it must also be possible to make a lot of noise within the space without disturbing others. The SchoolParasite must be able to serve as a bandstand or stage for performances. Naturally, storage space is also required for the musical instruments.

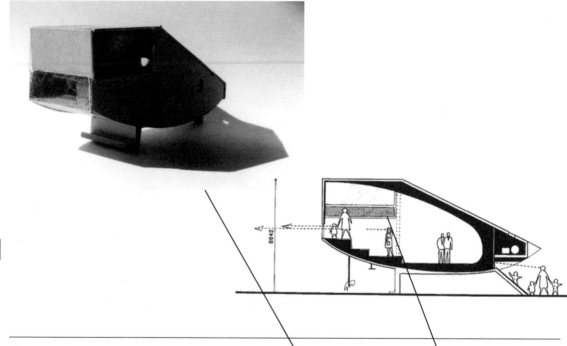

Alex van de Beld from ONIX has designed an exciting animal: it stands on two legs like a bird, its outward appearance is sturdy and angular like a bulldog and in its tail is a staircase that forms the entrance. The space under the belly is tall enough to play in or to sit out of the rain on the legs, which are also benches. The belly of the magical beast is an egg-shaped music and dance classroom made of wood, with different levels in the form of wide stages upon which you can sit. The windows are placed at a child's eye level. The tail contains storage space for musical instruments.
This SchoolParasite can also be used for other creative school subjects, as well as for performances, parent courses and parent evenings. Just as in the design by Christoph Seyferth, the space may be used after school for neighborhood activities. Because much consideration has been given to its acoustics, it could also be used by the local musical society and music school.

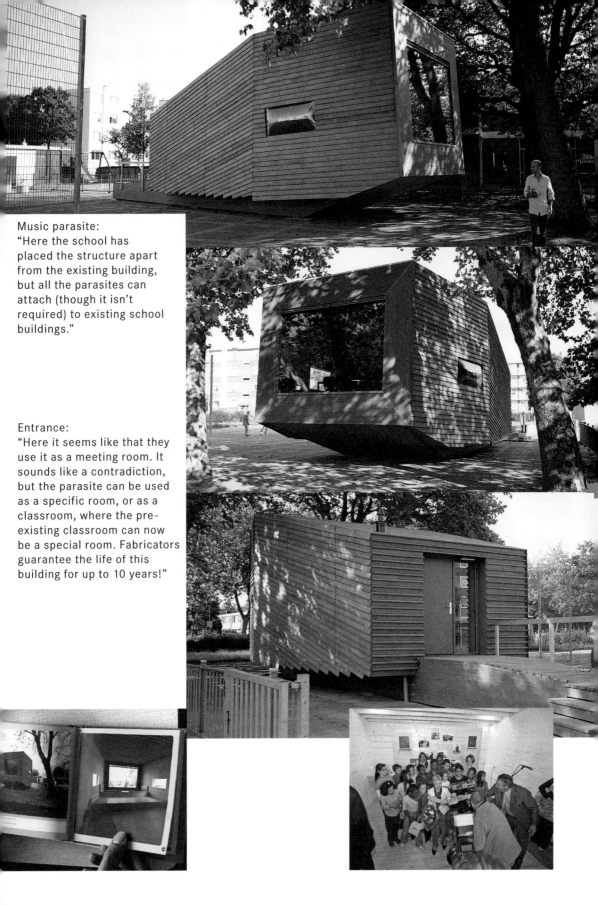

Music parasite:
"Here the school has placed the structure apart from the existing building, but all the parasites can attach (though it isn't required) to existing school buildings."

Entrance:
"Here it seems like that they use it as a meeting room. It sounds like a contradiction, but the parasite can be used as a specific room, or as a classroom, where the pre-existing classroom can now be a special room. Fabricators guarantee the life of this building for up to 10 years!"

School Parasite 3 : Bloern (Flower) > Designed by Barend Koolhaas

WORKSPACES The schools need room providing individual workspaces for the children, teachers and supervisors. Some children require extra supervision (e.g. social work, tutoring or speech therapy). If feasible, the schools always prefer to provide these services within the school, ensuring the student a greater level of accessibility that might otherwise be greatly reduced if these services were located elsewhere. Additional space is also required for support staff, as well as for more frequent and closer contact with parents.

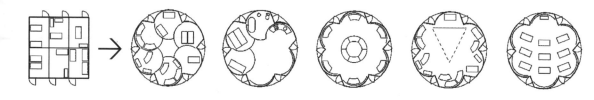

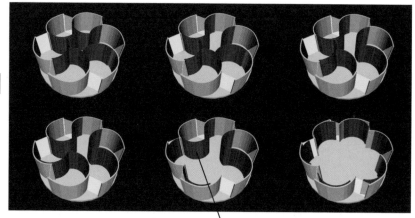

Barend Koolhaas from OI has designed a SchoolParasite in the form of a flower, in which simple and distinct workspaces can be created. The round building, nine metres in diameter, consists of six crescent-shaped flexible work-spaces. Each of these spaces is constructed of one long and one short, slightly bent panel. The short panels are <u>immobile</u>; they form the outer wall as well as the supporting structure. The long panels can each be pushed back bit by bit, in order to create larger spaces as needed. Many different configurations are possible. If all the panels are slid completely open, the space takes on the shape of a flower. As desired, the flower can be either attached to the school or stand free.

"This parasite is connected to the existing school building."

"This is a multi-use parasite. The plan can be varied a lot."

"The interior is very curious, especially the effect of the top-light. I've seen it like that."

TO CONCLUDE: THE DOMAIN OF HOOGVLIET

What will happen to Hoogvliet once all our projects will have been realized? Will the result differ fundamentally from the outcome of revitalization schemes in other New Towns? Or will our efforts prove to be but incidents that are bound to drown in the vast reconstruction work carried out by the official planning bureaucracies? Are they but romantic visions illustrating the merits of an old New Town? Is it at all possible for a small organization like ours to alter the course of these bureaucracies, as WiMBY! claims it can? Probably, the Domain of Hoogvliet will be the ultimate test case. All that WiMBY! has stood for during the last four years culminates in this project. The Domain of Hoogvliet is a Summer Park intended to provide recreation and entertainment. It is situated in the green buffer between Hoogvliet and the highway in the periphery of the 'oil' neighborhood. It comprises several components that have been developed in close cooperation with various groups of people in Hoogvliet: a tree collection, a pet cemetery, a natural playground, sports fields and a Villa. The local inhabitants not only initiated all these amenities, they will also be engaged in building, managing and maintaining them. In the park itself there are spaces for all kinds of activities: there are picnic and barbecue tables, as well as a pond for paddling. In the center of the Domain, the villa acts as an eye-catcher. It has been designed by the London based firm of FAT architects that also planned the park. Its character is purely narrative. The ornamental facades show elements that refer to the original village: green Hoogvliet, the chimney of the Shell refinery that triggered the idea to build Hoogvliet with the geometrical facades of 1950s architecture. It is a Venturian decorated shed containing the symbols and signs of a popular and recognizable visual language that can be easily understood by anyone.

Even for the fleeting passers-by, the need for a facility like the Domain is easily recognized, for in Hoogvliet little ever happens. The shopping mall boasts of a brasserie where one can have a coffee, but for younger people there is absolutely nothing to do, least of all during evenings and nights. The Villa will change this. Here, there will be musical performances, plays will be enacted and family celebrations can take place. Like the park, the Villa has something to offer everyone.

By keeping ourselves submerged in the wonderful world of Hoogvliet and engaged in the neverending pursuit of its inherent creative forces, we believe WiMBY! can contribute to a renaissance of the old New Town. Hoogvliet's negative image of a city inhabited by a dull NiMBY! population will be transformed into the positive image of a city with a peculiar mix of young and elderly people, people from the Netherlands Antilles, nature, industry, a place that makes its inhabitants proud and its visitors curious.

"No one had ever thought of making a park here before, or of bringing together all the local clubs and local leisure organizations together in one park."

Festival 16-17 August 2003 performance stage.
"Sam Jacob of FAT architects drew up a very cheap Potemkin façade of the park. We wanted to work with him because we thought he was the only architect capable of working on this kind of popular level in a very serious but necessarily commercial way. In a strange way, we have chosen a foreign architect for our most local project."

Festival 21-22 August 2004.
Photo: Maarten Laupman.

"For us the festival was a way to bring the park into existence in the minds of this whole community. It was a completely different way of realizing a big project, since we didn't go through all the layers of top-down planning, but the only way to do it was through popular imagination."

"We made brochures, posters and organized a Heerlijkheid Festival in this empty downtown square."

"One of our biggest schemes that was actually realized is a recreation park, a non profit Theme park celebrating the dreams of Hoogvliet. The Heerlijkheid Hoogvliet. It contains things as diverse as a beach, an open-air cinema, a party hall and a pet cemetery. In order to present it to the people of Hoogvliet we did not publish it, build a model, or make a video. We organized a party, and built the facades of the park in wood and cardboard, so that for two days a simulation of the park as a décor and as an event could be tried out and sampled by the public. 40,000 people showed up in two days, danced to the hip hop concerts, rode ponies, barbecued, had their hair braided and suggested changes to the plan. There we stood, pinching each other to make sure we were not dreaming. "So this is urban planning in the 21st century? My god!"

A Harbour in Denmark, 2004

Pearl of the Harbour

> SØREN HELL HANSEN, ROLAND MEIER, STEEN PALSBØLL, CLAUS PEDER PEDERSEN

Danish harbours have undergone a tremendous transformation in recent years. The functions of trade and transportation that used to dominate these areas are disappearing as the harbours develop into new urban and recreational areas.

While these developments create exciting and positive potential for Danish cities, they also present a distinct challenge. Alongside the urban functions overtaking the harbour, there is a risk of losing the unique characteristics and feel of the industrial harbour.

The city's harbour is no longer the main link to the world beyond; the great vessels, towering constructions, raw materials and the smell of the sea that have always characterised the harbour are disappearing, along with many of the exotic and fantastic qualities of the original port.

A Pearl of the Harbour is a mobile floating vessel, bringing contemporary activities and adventures to Danish ports. Its focus is the new role the harbour will have in the present and ongoing development of the country's cities.

The vessel is built on an adaptable base or raft of floating concrete elements, fitted out with a choice of distinctive superstructures designed to accommodate various programmatic and architectural expressions.

A Pearl of the Harbour forges interaction between city and harbour by introducing new cultural, commercial and recreational aspects. The water remains an active element within the de-industrialized harbour. A Pearl of the Harbour is constructed using contemporary methods and materials. The harbour is a unique place where structure and texture are emphatically different from the rest of the city.

STRUCTURES ON FLOATING CONCRETE ELEMENTS

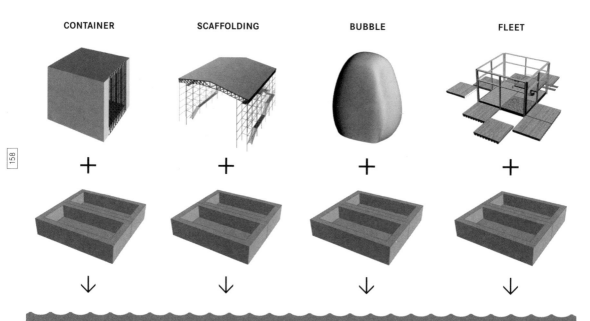

CONTAINER   SCAFFOLDING   BUBBLE   FLEET

FLOATING ELEMENT   A Pearl of the Harbour is situated on one or several connected floating elements. The floating element (an E&A HUBB® concrete foundation) is constructed of steel-reinforced, non-degradable, seawater-resistant concrete, measuring 7 x 14 m. This is a common, tested and inexpensive construction approved by the Danish Maritime Authority.

The separate elements can be connected at both ends and at the sides to produce custom-made floating elements to suit any need, programme or budget.

A Pearl of the Harbour can be moored in various ways depending on local conditions and requirements: close to the quay for easy access or out in the harbour to create the greatest visual impact.

50 CITIES – ONE PLACE   A Pearl of the Harbour is a seagoing vessel, which grants it a degree of independence from local planning regulations. This mobility results in quick assembly as a temporary or permanent element of the city. The vessel may focus on the future development of the harbour or function as a permanent addition to the existing city. Placement may emphasize a particular spot or circulate around different harbours, reappearing in an area or at recurring events. A Pearl of the Harbour could, for instance, go on a summer cruise in the archipelago south of Fyn, anchoring in a different harbour every weekend. Another option would be relocating it in and around Copenhagen's harbour to create various focal points. www.stougaard-aluscan.com/forside.html

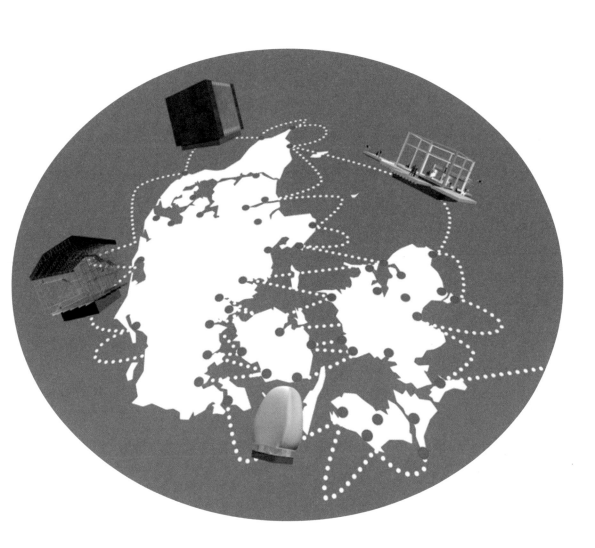

The Container is a heated, ventilated space owing its name to the crude steel containers used for transporting goods often stacked in modern-day ports. The great vaulted space is a reference to the vast spaces used for constructing the hulls of ships with overwhelming space, structures and large openings for light.

The Scaffolding is an open deck covered by a steel construction resembling the traditional cranes and masts common to the harbour.

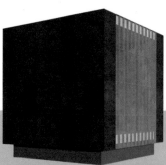

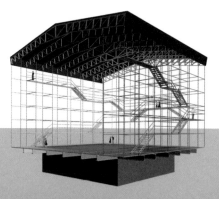

Gross area: 650 m²
Heated area: 430 m² (2 staff toilets, changing rooms, storage rooms and technical installations)
Unheated area: 220 m²
Maximum occupancy: 100 persons
Geometry: 16 x 16 x 16 metres
Product no: 03HP-B-CONTAINEREN
Price: 1,156,770 €

Gross area: 620 m²
Heated area: 100 m² (2 staff toilets, changing rooms, storage rooms, technical installations)
Unheated area: 500 m²
Maximum occupancy: 100 persons
Geometry: 20 x 20 x 20 metres
Product no: 03HP-A-STILLADSET
Price: 1,416,680 €

BUBBLE

FLEET

The Bubble is a distinctive, pneumatic, tent-like construction. This strangely foreign, sculptural shape evokes visions of both underwater jellyfish and full sails.

The Fleet is an assortment of smaller rafts distributed around the primary floating element. The Fleet includes maritime references to rafts and floating timber. Each raft reflects the various parts of the mooring of a vessel (deck, beach, dock, lookout tower and ferry ramps), all in surprisingly surrealistic versions.

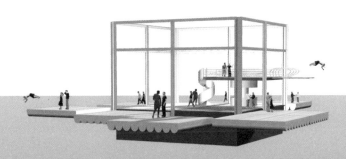

Gross area: 620 m²
Heated area: 90 m²
Unheated area: 470 m²
Partly heated area (area within the bubble): 400 m²
Maximum occupancy: 100 persons
Geometry: 15 x 15 x 30 metres
Ø: 19 m
Product no: 03HP-C-BOBLEN
Price: 1,261,650 €

Gross area: 780 m²
Heated area: 90 m² (2 staff toilets, changing rooms, 4 public toilets, storage rooms and technical installations)
Unheated area: 690 m²
Maximum occupancy: 100 persons
Geometry: 14 x 14 x 10 metres
Product no: 03HP-D-FLÅDEN
Price: 583,290 €

CONTAINER
Exhibitions and Studios
Theatre and Concert space / Film Forum
Lecture hall, Community Centre and Exhibition space
Market with stalls and viewing platform / Convenience store
Children's centre and Playhouse
Hostel, Dormitory and Office space

SCAFFOLDING
Theatre and Concert space
Cinema and Film Forum
Market with stalls
Exhibitions
Seafood restaurant

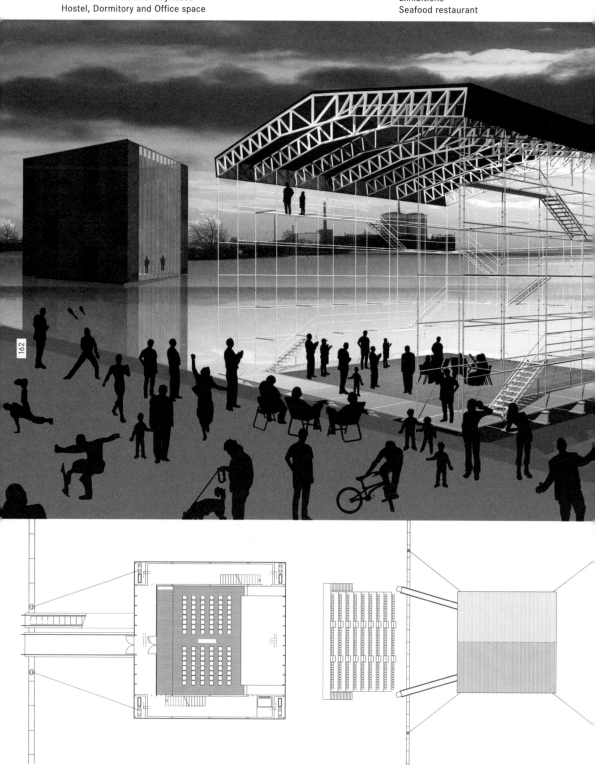

BUBBLE
Night club and Lounge
Internet café and Gallery
Design fair and Art exhibition
Community Service Centre and Exhibition of the city
Children's fair and Activities
Basketball court
3 Badminton courts

FLEET
Recreational area (summer)
Café
Beach
Kayak rental
Diving platform
Children's pool

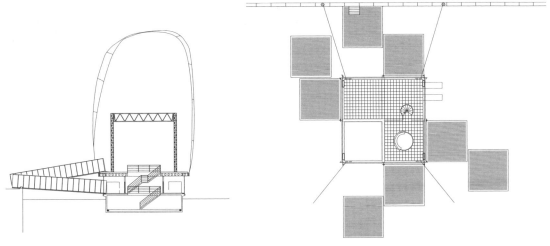

Sundby Harbour, Copenhagen, 2004

164

Maritime Youth House > PLOT

The concept of the project is based on the discovery that pollution of the site's soil was caused by heavy metals and was, therefore, stable; if we didn't reach the ground, we wouldn't have to clean it. As a result, instead of using a quarter of the project's budget to clean the soil, we decided to lay a wooden deck over the entire site, enabling us to spend money on architecture, programme and effect rather than on invisible waste.

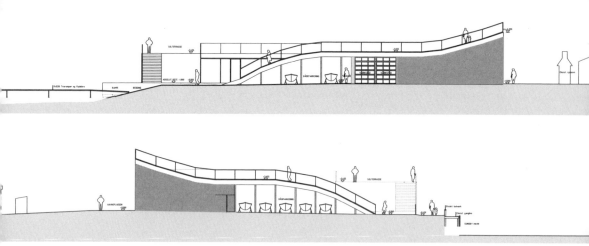

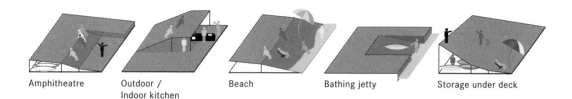

Amphitheatre Outdoor / Indoor kitchen Beach Bathing jetty Storage under deck

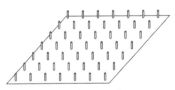

Piles driven into the ground

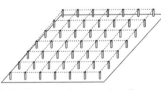

Grid of beams in between the piles

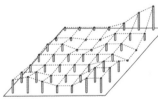

Piles of varying heights =
Landscape of possibilities

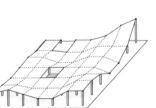

Possibilities of actitivities

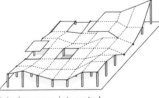

Interior space integrated

Existing trees and nature

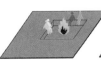

Bonfire pit

Fishing pond

Bathing bassin

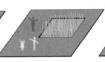

Rootzone garden

Pre-existing tree

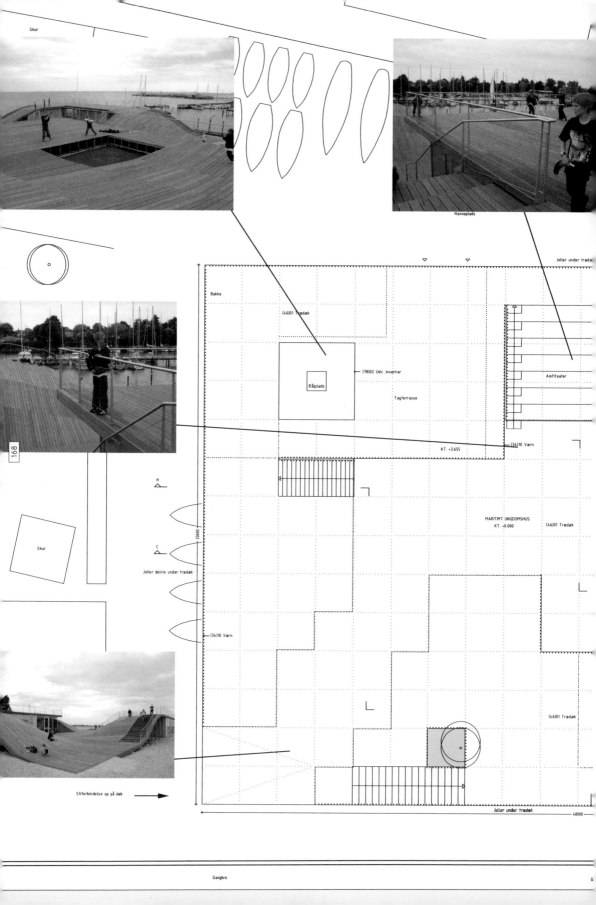

Skur

Havneplads

168

Bakke

(46)01 Trædæk

(78)02 Udv. inventar

Bålplads

Tagterrasse

Amfiteater

(34)10 Værn

KT. +3.655

H

MARITIMT UNGDOMSHUS
KT. +0.000

(46)01 Trædæk

C

Skur

Joller delvis under trædæk

(34)10 Værn

(46)01 Trædæk

Stiforbindelse op på dæk →

Joller under trædæk

48000

Gangbro

G

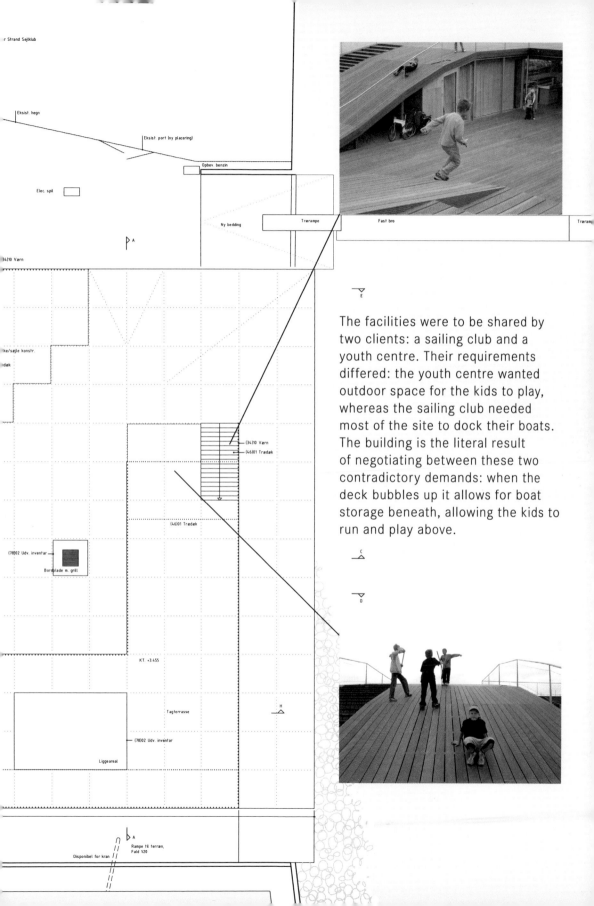

r Strand Sejlklub

Eksist. hegn

Eksist. port (ny placering)

Opbev. benzin

Elec. spil

Ny bedding

Trærampe

Fast bro

Trærampe

A

34)10 Værn

ke/søjle konstr.

ndæk

(34)10 Værn
(46)01 Trædæk

(46)01 Trædæk

(78)02 Udv. inventar

Bordplade m. grill

KT. +3.455

Tagterrasse

H

(78)02 Udv. inventar

Liggeareal

A

Rampe til terræn,
Fald 120

Disponibel for kran

E

The facilities were to be shared by
two clients: a sailing club and a
youth centre. Their requirements
differed: the youth centre wanted
outdoor space for the kids to play,
whereas the sailing club needed
most of the site to dock their boats.
The building is the literal result
of negotiating between these two
contradictory demands: when the
deck bubbles up it allows for boat
storage beneath, allowing the kids to
run and play above.

C

D

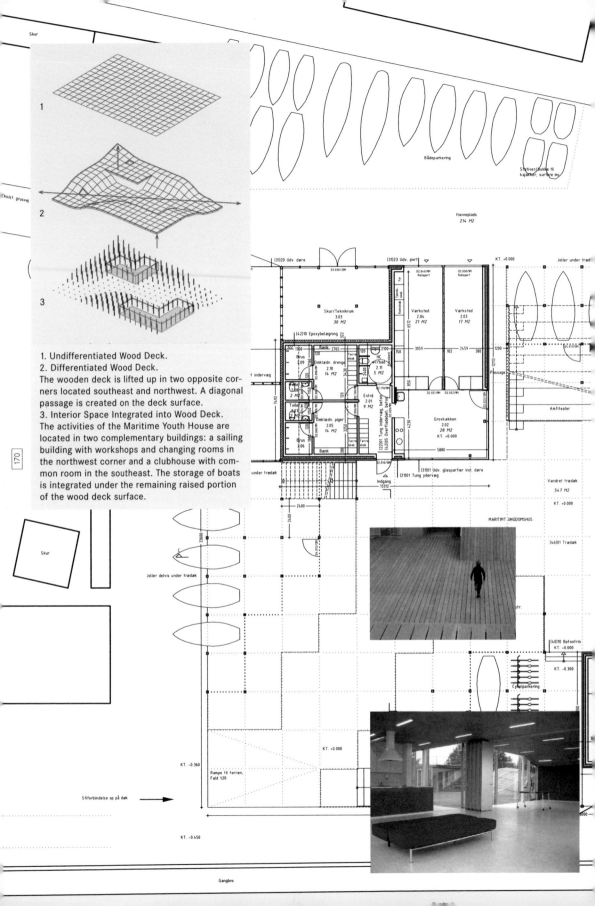

1. Undifferentiated Wood Deck.
2. Differentiated Wood Deck.
The wooden deck is lifted up in two opposite corners located southeast and northwest. A diagonal passage is created on the deck surface.
3. Interior Space Integrated into Wood Deck.
The activities of the Maritime Youth House are located in two complementary buildings: a sailing building with workshops and changing rooms in the northwest corner and a clubhouse with common room in the southeast. The storage of boats is integrated under the remaining raised portion of the wood deck surface.

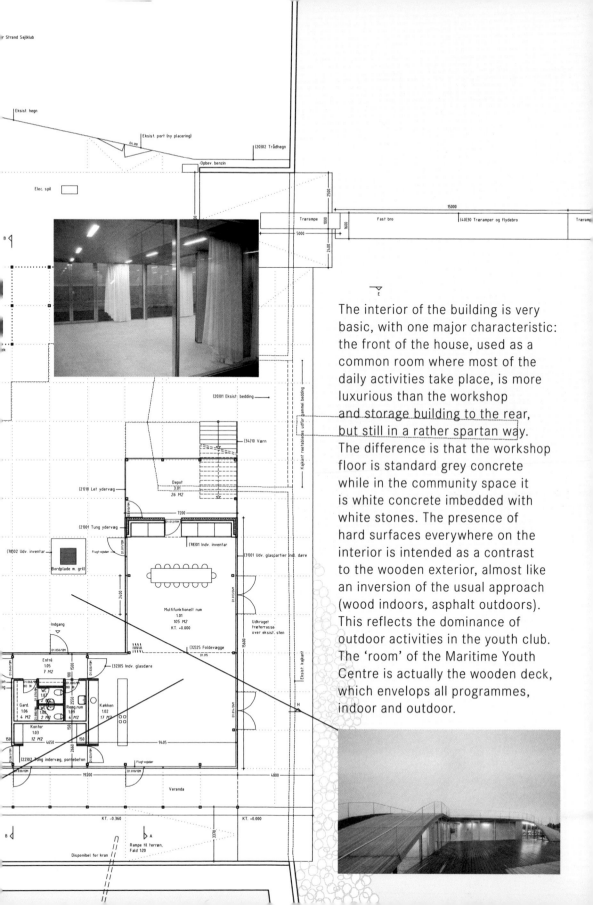

ir Strand Sejlklub

Eksist. hegn

Eksist. port (ny placering)

(20)02 Trådhegn

Opbev. benzin

Elec. spil

15000

Trærampe

Fast bro

(40)30 Træramper og flydebro

Træramp

E

The interior of the building is very basic, with one major characteristic: the front of the house, used as a common room where most of the daily activities take place, is more luxurious than the workshop and storage building to the rear, but still in a rather spartan way. The difference is that the workshop floor is standard grey concrete while in the community space it is white concrete imbedded with white stones. The presence of hard surfaces everywhere on the interior is intended as a contrast to the wooden exterior, almost like an inversion of the usual approach (wood indoors, asphalt outdoors). This reflects the dominance of outdoor activities in the youth club. The 'room' of the Maritime Youth Centre is actually the wooden deck, which envelops all programmes, indoor and outdoor.

(20)01 Eksist. bedding

Kajkant reetableds udfor gammel bedding

(34)10 Værn

(21)10 Let ydervæg

Depot
3.01
26 M2

7200

(21)01 Tung ydervæg

(78)01 Indv. inventar

(78)02 Udv. inventar

Flugt vejeder

Bordplade m. grill

(31)01 Udv. glaspartier incl. døre

Multifunktionelt rum
1.01
105 M2
KT. +0.000

Udkraget
træterrasse
over eksist. sten

Indgang

Eksist. kajkant

(32)25 Foldevægge

Entré
1.05
7 M2

(32)05 Indv. glasdøre

WC
1.07

Gard.
1.06
4 M2

Reng.rum
1.04

Køkken
1.02
17 M2

Kontor
1.03
12 M2

Flugt vejeder

(22)02 Tung indervæg, portebeton

19200

4800

Veranda

KT. -0.360

KT. +0.000

A

Rampe til terræn,
Fald 120

Disponibel for kran

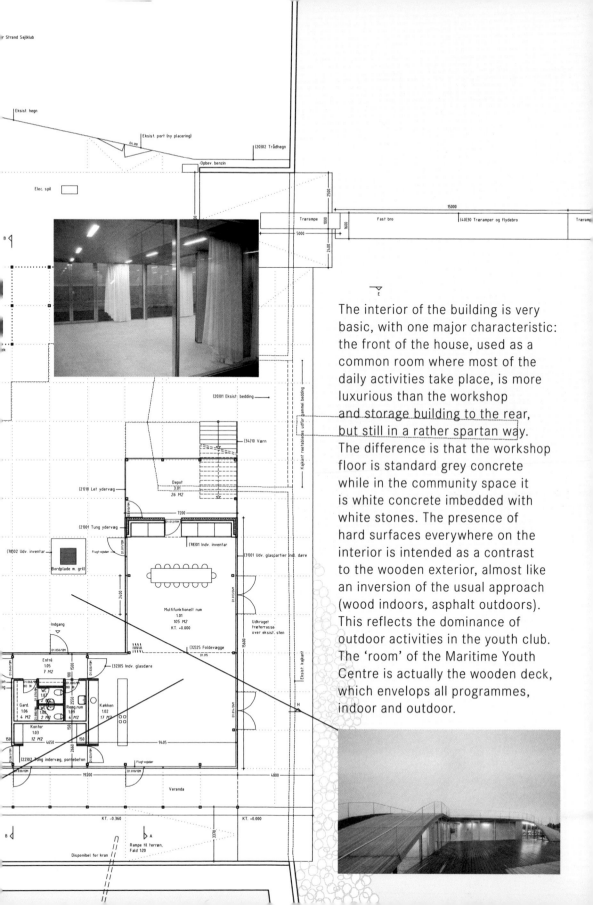

MARITIME YOUTH HOUSE. SUNDBY HARBOUR, COPENHAGEN. DENMARK   www.plot.dk

<u>Client</u>: Kvarterløft Governmental City Renewal Project, Lokale OG Anlægsfonden, The Urban Development Fond. <u>Design</u>: PLOT. <u>Project team</u>: Bjarke Ingels, Julien De Smedt, Annette Jensen, Finn Nørkjær, Henning Stüben, Jørn Jensen, Mads H Lund, Marc Jay, Nina Ter-Borch. <u>Consultants</u>: Birch & Krogboe A/S, Jesper Gudman (Struktur). <u>Type</u>: Invited competition, 1st Prize. <u>Size</u>: 2,000 m². <u>Budget</u>: 1,170,000 €. <u>Status</u>: completion February 2004.

Magasin du Nord department store > PLOT

Copenhagen is suffering the same fate as most other historic cities. The well-conserved city is a nostalgic image of the city that once was but does not reflect the city's current content, activities, desires or demands. The ultimate consequence of this conservationism is a phenomenon known as façadism: urban transformation is concealed by preserving the façades of buildings as shells, while the inner organs are constantly refurbished. Urban life remains captive inside an increasingly inadequate container.

All our dreams that do not fit within the template of the historic city are banished to life in the suburbs, where historic heritage is less of a burden and space is more abundant.

In order to prevent inner cities from petrifying into well-kept museums of the past and to breathe life into historical surroundings, we need to invent new ways of sharing space – to give both old and new, high and low, progressive and popular a share of the city.

Høje Torv, Copenhagen, 2005

The story of Høje Torv (High Square) shows how a variety of different interest groups and disciplines have influenced and inhabited our work. Høje Torv is the result of a chain of coincident events: the merger of a bank with a credit union, a theoretical project in Manhattan, the opening of a new market place in an old department store, a heat wave, the extension of a parking lot and the opening of a new underground. The story of Høje Torv is the story of how these conditions were interwoven, step by step, and how each was apportioned its share of an architectural site.

Høje Torv attempts to overcome this conservation of the inner city not by changing the way it looks, but by changing the way we look at it. Høje Torv constitutes a new level of urban space with views over and across the city that, out of sight, can host the multiplicity that the historic city has neither the guts to promote nor the space to accommodate.

AUGUST 2002 An aerial photograph of Copenhagen reveals that Magasin's rooftop is the largest flat-elevated surface in the entire city. It sits right in the town centre with views of the Royal Square and the pedestrian shopping streets. We called Magasin and asked what they thought about the idea of laying a 3,000 square metre public square on their private roof. A planned extension of Magasin's car park, integrated with the new square, would in principle allow users to hail a taxi 26 metres over the city. The project is named Høje Torv.

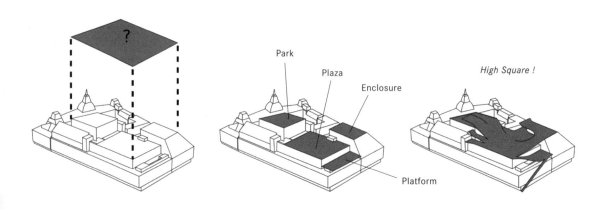

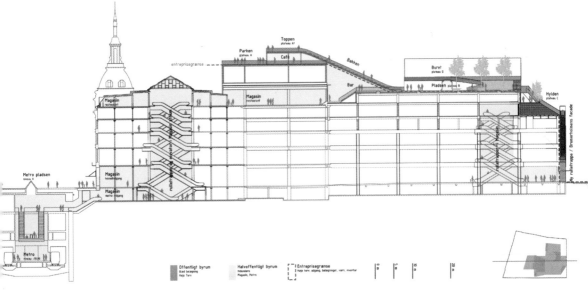

JUNE 2005   Hundreds of Danes and tourists enjoy the sun on Høje Torv. Some lie on the grass and look at the clouds sailing by, others point out significant landmarks in the city skyline, such as Arne Jacobsen's SAS Hotel, the Marble Church or the recently opened Opera House. Newcomers emerge from the Underground station and pop up in the square. Some, after shopping at Magasin, sip refreshments on the arena steps under the clear, sunny sky. Others find the sun so strong that they happily give in to their shopper's instinct and head downstairs into Magasin – after all, you can always do with a pair of shades on Høje Torv. JULIEN DE SMEDT AND BJARKE INGELS

HØJE TORV (HIGH SQUARE), COPENHAGEN. DENMARK   www.plot.dk

Client: Magasin du Nord, Realdania Foundation, Copenhagen City Council. Design: PLOT. Project team: Bjarke Ingels, Julien De Smedt, Finn Nørkjær, Henrik Juul Nielsen, Jesper Wichmann, Thomas Christoffersen, Xavi Pavia Pages. Consultants: Birch & Krogboe A/S. Photographers: Simon Ladefoged, Jakob Galtt. Area: 3,000 m². Budget: 3,900,000 €.

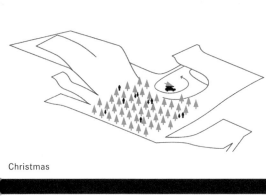

Christmas

Summer

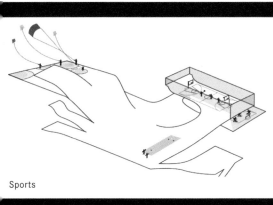

Sports

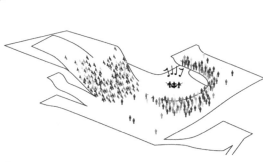

Festival

Islands Brygge, Copenhagen, 2003

Harbour Bath

Copenhagen's harbour is undergoing a transformation from an industrial and traffic junction to becoming the city's cultural and social centre. The Harbour Bath design emerged from the desire to extend the surrounding park into the water and the practical requirements of accessibility, safety and programmatic demand. The Harbour Bath realises the transition from land to water in the form of a terraced landscape.

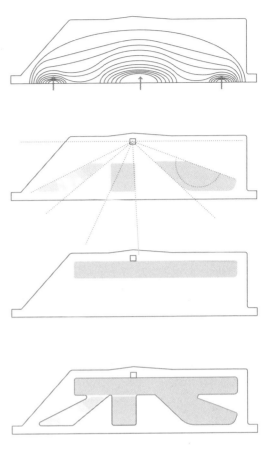

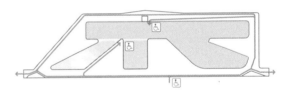

For many years, the harbour's waters have been polluted. The Municipality of Copenhagen has worked for ten years to clean up the water, turning it into a place where local people and tourists can enjoy swimming. It has a continuous wooden deck to provide barrier-free access to all.

COPENHAGEN HARBOUR BATH, COPENHAGEN. DENMARK www.plot.dk

<u>Client</u>: Copenhagen City Council / Lokale & Anlægsfonden. <u>Design</u>: PLOT. <u>Project team</u>: Julien De Smedt, Bjarke Ingels, Christian Finderup, Finn Nørkjær, Henning Stüben, Ingrid Serristlev, Jakob Møller, Marc Jay. <u>Engineer</u>: Birch Og Krogboe. <u>Entrepeneur</u>: CC Design. <u>Type</u>: Commision. <u>Completion</u>: June 2003. <u>Floor area</u>: 1,600 m². <u>Budget</u>: 520,000 €.

Spree River, Berlin, 2004

Badeschiff / Swimming Ship > AMP architects + Gil Wilk + Susanne Lorenz

The Spreebrücke project approaches the 'bridge' concept from a literal and figurative viewpoint. The 'bridge' is not only seen as a connection between two points, it also forms a connecting line within the city. Spreebrücke is the bridge that makes the river Spree an inhabitable place.

Spreebrücke is made up of four elements: a barge-type boat for bathing, a beach on the riverbank, timber platforms used as connecting elements and a container. All the components may be transported on the barge and together form a mobile Spree-Pool which is not fixed to any given point but can be set up in different places.

Spreebrücke is a meeting point and a place of communication. It is an inhabitable bridge for the Spree river. The city of Spreebrücke set out to promote awareness of the river and its qualities within the city. Like the first drop of clean water, the project reintroduces the idea of swimming to the Spree and revives an old tradition. In the late 19th century, there were fifteen private swimming pools along the Spree, including four in the stretch between Jannowitzbrücke and Elsenbrücke. These pools consisted of a specially designated stretch the Spree river itself, or of clean water pools called *Badeschiffe* (bathing boats). As the city's industry developed during the late-nineteenth century, growing levels of pollution led to the closure of the baths prior to World War I.

In remembrance of this story, we chose a site near the Eastside Gallery as our first stop for the Spree-Pool.

Old swimming pool on the river. It was closed for the pollution of the water.

BATHING BOAT   The barge turned swimming pool is a medium-sized transport craft known as a *Schubleichte*, which is widely used on the Spree. The upper parts of the barge have been removed and new fittings installed. The 'pool' is filled by means of piping located at the bottom of the pool and designed to produce a homogeneous surface. The pool is emptied from beneath the new construction. The piping terminates in a filter that, along with the other services, is housed in the container. The surface of the water is highlighted by a system of coloured lighting (blue/green) fixed onto the inside walls of the pool. The boat is attached to the embankment by two flexible metal frames. On the Spree, the boat highlights a stretch of water and transforms the activity of swimming in the river into an attraction. In winter the bathing boat can be used as an ice-skating rink.

BRIDGE   The bridge connects the beach and the swimming pool. It responds to the nautical form of a boat and consists of two horizontal timber platforms interconnected by two walkways. The structure may be quickly assembled and dismounted. Large vertical trunks moor the ends to the site. This flexiblily enables great mobility and the bridge is easily adapted to different site conditions. The bridge is moored to the wall of the embankment and simply rests on the riverbed. Entrance to the swimming pool can be monitored.

BEACH   Situated on the riverbank, the beach is made of clean white sand lit by ground lights at night. The bar and changing rooms, also built of timber, are situated on it.

190

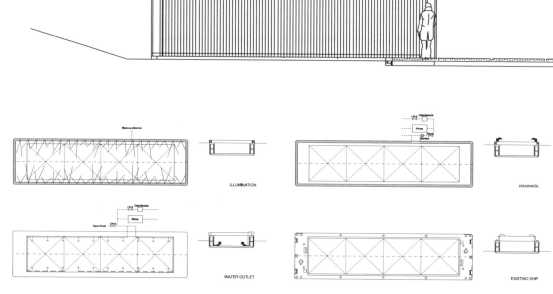

ILLUMINATION

DRAINAGE

WATER OUTLET

EXISTING SHIP

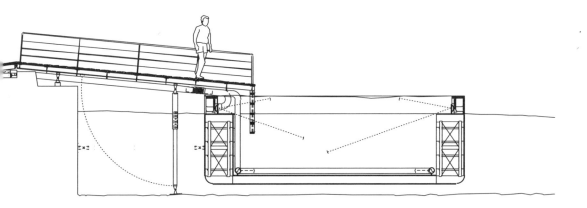

Bridges + beach + swimming pool stand right next to the urban area, adjacent to brick buildings that are currently used as a bus depot. The swimming pool is 32.5 m x 8 m x 2 m and filled with 400 tons of water.

BADESCHIFF

Architects: AMP arquitectos S.L., Artengo-Menis–Pastrana, Susanne Lorenz. Assistant architect: Gil Wilk.
Curator: Heike Catherina Müller. Structure: Juan José Gallardo. Construction: José Perera Marrero.

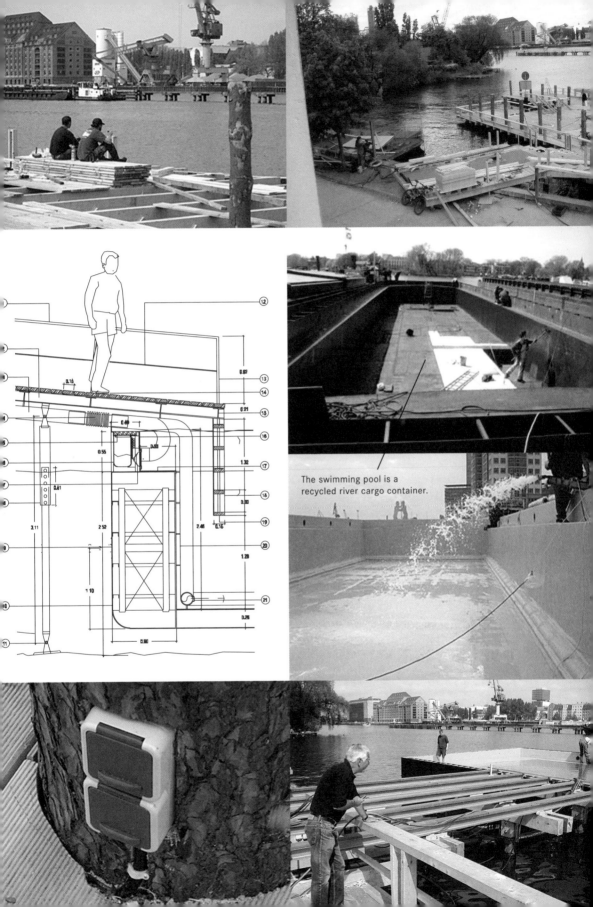

The swimming pool is a
recycled river cargo container.

Open from 8 a.m. to midnight, the pool is illuminated with an orange glow at night. During colder seasons, swimmers can still enjoy the pool, which is heated to 24 degrees Celcius.

Kanazawa, 2004

ARCHITECTURAL CONCEPT & DESIGN INFORMATION

The 21st Century Museum of Contemporary Art in Kanazawa stands in the city center on a site linking diverse but equally important city functions. Circular in form, with a diameter of 112.5 meters, the building has no front or back, leaving it free to be explored from all directions. While designed to offer accessibility from multiple points of entry, the circular plan also works in concert with keeping the overall building volume low, effectively mitigating the scale of the project and reducing the overly grand presence common to large institutions. In order to further encourage the multiplicity of approaches, the architects have intentionally resisted establishing a primary façade or entrance.

Programmatically, the project includes community gathering spaces, such as a library, lecture hall, and children's workshop, as well as museum spaces. The public and museum zones are organized to provoke interrelation, with the public spaces encircling the museum. Exhibition spaces are fragmented into numerous galleries that are embedded within the circulation. This approach offers specificity to the gallery spaces yet flexibility of museum routing, with multiple options for division into smaller exhibitions, expansion, or concentration of the ticketed areas. The scattered bulk of the galleries, as opposed to a conventional solution with one or a few great exhibition spaces, provide transparency, with views from the periphery into the center and vistas through the entire depth of the building. This transparency further helps to avoid the perception of the museum as a large, introverted mass.

Specificity of each gallery space is one advantage of the building concept that has been fully explored. Galleries vary in proportions and light conditions – from bright daylight cast through glass ceilings, to spaces with no natural light that range in height from four to twelve meters. Circulation spaces are designed to allow their use as additional exhibition areas. Four fully glazed internal courtyards, each unique in character, provide ample daylight to the center and a fluid border between the public zones and museum zones.

While it is a very large building, the building retains a bright, open and free feeling.
It provides an unforgettable aesthetic environment; one which will point towards the possibilities of continued creativity in the future.

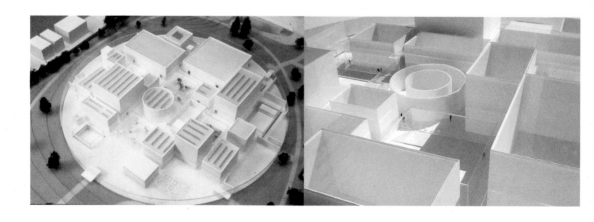

MUSEUM CONCEPT

The 21st Century Museum of Contemporary Art in Kanazawa presents a model for a 21st century art museum with a dual design focus.

The first is the integration of the design of the museum space with the program. The result of a four year collaboration between museum staff and architect, SANAA is a "device" that transcends its function as a museum space to provide information and programs offering a wide range of experiences for visitors, engineering their awareness.

The variously proportioned rooms scattered throughout the circle, a model based on the concept of an island chain or urban space, signify the centers that generate values originating in the poor distribution of decentrism and polycentrism, and in remote regions. The transparent corridors that offer a clear view of the entire museum space encourage "coexistence" in which individuals remain autonomous while sharing personal space with others. The design, which allows visitors to create customized routes through the museum, combined with the flexible gallery spaces, adaptable to every type of media, guarantees that the trans-border diversity of the programs held in this space. The intention behind all of these elements is to stimulate the visitor's emerging awareness.

20th century Modernism was driven by the three M's: Man, Money and Materialism. With the replacement of these three M's with the three C's: Consciousness, Collective Intelligence and Co-existence, new forms of expression are now beginning to appear. The 21st Century Museum of Contemporary Art in Kanazawa is an enormous catalytic "device", whose purpose is to convey the "psychological products" of these three C's to visitors, to ensure their effect and to revitalize everyone who comes into contact with the museum.

The second aspect, or design focus, was the view of "the initiator" as transitional and coexistent. In the past, the curator, in the role of art specialist, acted as the "initiator" by determining the value of art, had the final word on new acquisitions and was responsible for all other activities. Programs that encourage visitors to act more as initiators, deconstructionist programs and programs focusing on destroying the perception of "self", have been incorporated into 21st Century Museum of Contemporary Art, Kanazawa's range of activities. If, as Beuys said, "everyone is an artist", this museum dreams of a time when anyone can participate in determining value and show works based on their own criteria; a time when anyone can act as curator. The resources of the 21st Century Museum of Contemporary Art in Kanazawa become a "device" that chooses to promote a perspective focused on values that are different from those of Western modernism, committed to a deep and strong involvement with society and the world at large and to generating future values still yet undetermined.

21ST CENTURY MUSEUM OF CONTEMPORARY ART, KANAZAWA   www.sanaa.co.jp / www.kanazawa21.jp

Location: Hirosaka, Kanazawa City, Ishikawa Prefecture, Japan. Client: Kanazawa City. Design: Kazuyo Sejima, Ryue Nishizawa/SANAA. Structure: Sasaki Structural Consultants. Construction Period: March 2002 - September 2004. Plot area: 36,964.5 m². Floor Area: 27,920 m². Floor Number: 2 Floors on the ground + 2 Floors under the ground. Structure: Reinforced Concrete + Steel Structure. Dimension: diameter 113m, maximum height 14.9m, eaves height 4.651m. Photographs: 21st Century Museum of Contemporary Art, Kanazawa.

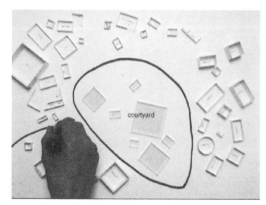

From the video for the exhibition "Recent Projects" at Aedes Gallery, Berlin.

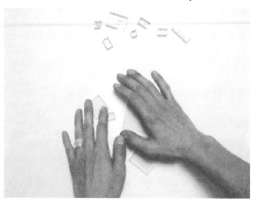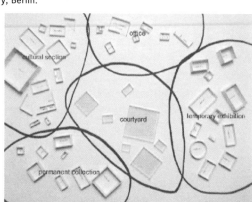

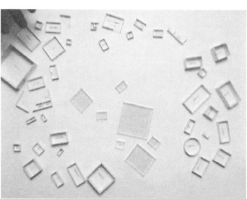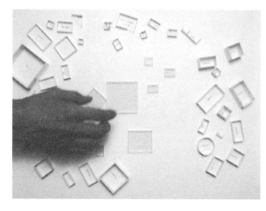

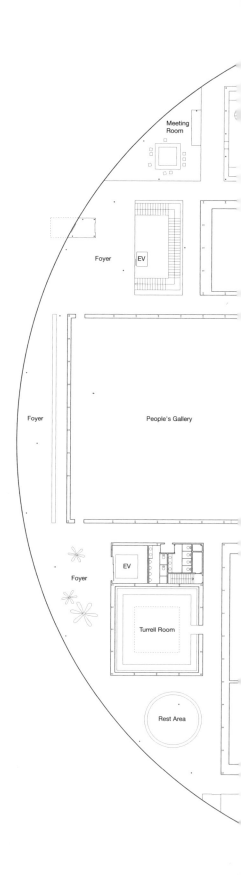

202

8th of October 2004, opening day of the exhibition.

Administrative Office

Curatorial Office

Long-Term Project

Info Terminal

...ater 21

Rest Area

Courtyard

Gallery 8

Museum Shop

Design Gallery

...11

Gallery 12

Gallery 10

Gallery 9

Gallery 7

Cafe

...rea

Courtyard

Gallery 14

Courtyard

Foyer

Courtyard

EV

EV

Gallery 1

...13

Gallery 6

Lecture Hall

Gallery 5

Courtyard

Kapoor Room

...4

Rest Area

Gallery 3

Gallery 2

Rest Area

Library

Lounge

Kid's Studio

Museum open to the city like a park

21st Century Museum of Contemporary Art, Kanazawa is situated in the center of Kanazawa city. Anyone can drop by whenever they want. The museum is designed as a park where people can gather and meet with one another. The glass-made circle results in an ambiguous spatial definition, or kind of reversible membrane, through which visitors can sense each other's presence. The museum pays careful attention to its openness and brightness from the courtyards with skylights. The Museum, in order to meet various needs of visitors, also contains a shop and restaurant open during night hours. The aim of the museum is to create an atmosphere of "casualness," "enjoyment" and "accessibility".

The characteristics of architectural design

The circle = Multiple directions. The most visible characteristic of the museum is its form. The site, surrounded by three streets, is accessible from multiple directions, which inspired the circular plan. Anyone may enter the museum through at any entrance helping to facilitate accessibility a sense of closeness between the building and the city.

Horizontality = Location of facility

The exhibition rooms, restaurant and art library are located horizontally, helping to give the museum a spread out quality, allowing visitors were feel as though they were in the downtown area. The natural circulation of the museum provides clear views between different areas.

Transparency = Producing openness

The use of glass walls, on the interior and exterior, produces transparency and brightness. It also enhances a sense of encounter, an awareness of each other's presence, and unity among the visitors, be they inside or outside the building.

→ VERB

New city development can disrupt pre-existing neighborhood networks. This project by Kazuhiro Kojima attempts to redesign the naturally occurring housing typology found in crowded Asian cities. The architect wanted to create a prototype that would maintain the culture of density found in these cities, but achieve greater levels of comfort in their hot and humid climates. Individual housing units can be aggregated to create any sized apartment block, yet remain well-ventilated by the 'voids,' which encourage community interaction via auditory and visual exchange.

36 Streets, Hanoi, 2004

Space Block Hanoi Model > Kazuhiro Kojima

HANOI MODEL For the last five years, the project has been funded by the Japanese Government. The project team, formed mainly by Tokyo University and the Hanoi University of Architecture, brings together professionals from such varied fields as planning, history, structures and installations. The research project is now entering its final year with the construction of an experimental housing complex, scheduled for completion in February 2003. The aim of the project is to research a model type for residential areas with low impact on the environment in hot, humid climates, such as in Asia. The project team was based in Tokyo and the model housing was built in Hanoi.

BACKGROUND Population explosion. The field of study, South-East and Eastern Asia, is experiencing a tremendous population increase, which represents a strain on the environment, accompanied by the urban heat island phenomenon.

OBJECTIVES
1. To develop an 'anti-sprawl' city model in the form of a compact, low-rise, high-density city (1,000 people per hectare with a maximum height of 16 metres). This extreme condition is the present situation here in 36 Streets (the Old Quarter), Hanoi.
2. To produce a model architecture that is, as far as possible, independent of air-conditioning systems and therefore environmentally sustainable. Furthermore, this model architecture will also need to sustain the context of the city.

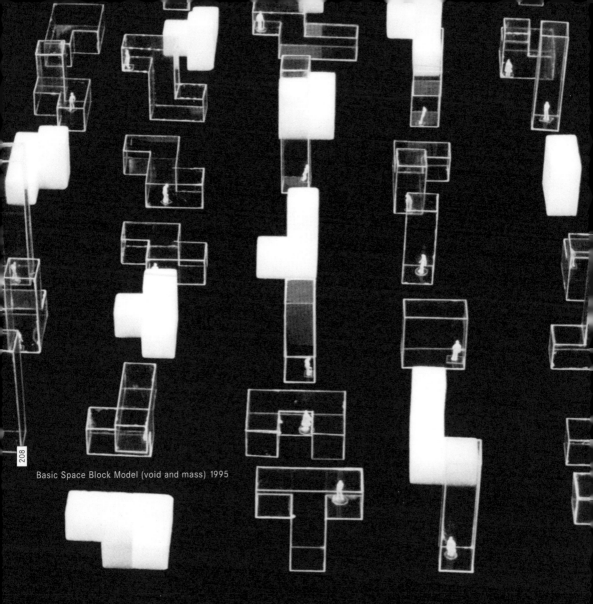

Basic Space Block Model (void and mass) 1995

METHOD: SPACE BLOCK   Space Block is a three-dimensional design tool that can be combined, like blocks, to study the complex composition of inside and outside space. Using this method, it is easy to visualize the entire three-dimensional porous space in the form of a void-mass ratio. The Basic Space Block (BSB) contains three to five cubes of interior space (white) or exterior space (transparent). Kazuhiro Kojima and Coelacanth Architects have used this method since 1993 to research, study and design highly complex three-dimensional space in Asian cities such as Tokyo, Hong Kong and Taipei, this time applying it to Hanoi.

90 % void	80 %	70 %	60 %	50 %	40 %	30 %	20 %	10 %

A set of Space Blocks used to visualize void to mass ratio 1997

Hong Kong Kowloon Model (1997)

Space Block Model: Taipei Model (1997)

Tokyo Kasumigaseki Model (1997)

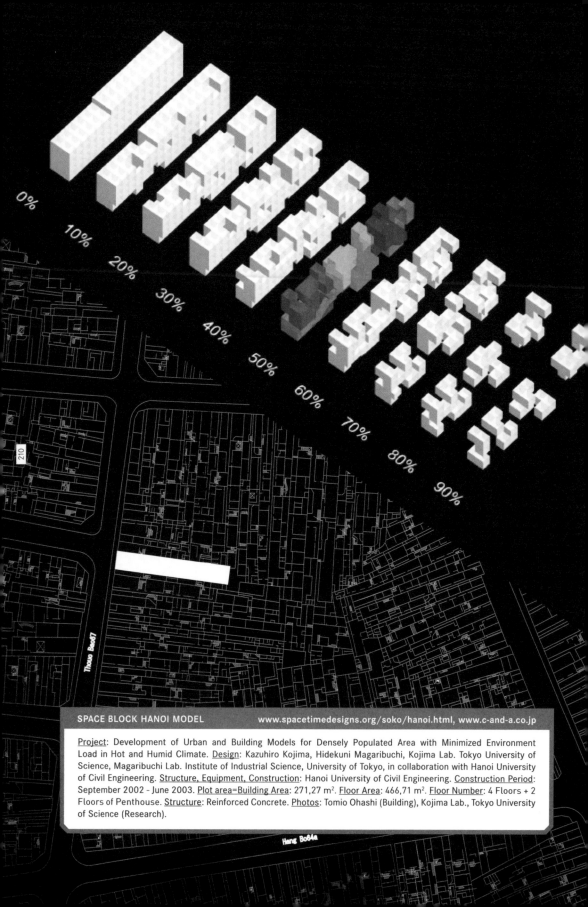

0% 10% 20% 30% 40% 50% 60% 70% 80% 90%

210

Thoue Bao57

Hang Bo64e

SPACE BLOCK HANOI MODEL www.spacetimedesigns.org/soko/hanoi.html, www.c-and-a.co.jp

Project: Development of Urban and Building Models for Densely Populated Area with Minimized Environment Load in Hot and Humid Climate. Design: Kazuhiro Kojima, Hidekuni Magaribuchi, Kojima Lab. Tokyo University of Science, Magaribuchi Lab. Institute of Industrial Science, University of Tokyo, in collaboration with Hanoi University of Civil Engineering. Structure, Equipment, Construction: Hanoi University of Civil Engineering. Construction Period: September 2002 - June 2003. Plot area=Building Area: 271,27 m². Floor Area: 466,71 m². Floor Number: 4 Floors + 2 Floors of Penthouse. Structure: Reinforced Concrete. Photos: Tomio Ohashi (Building), Kojima Lab., Tokyo University of Science (Research).

Each color represents one family. 6 families of 4-6 people yield 30 people in this entire building. (1000 people/ha).

Roof Plan | +12.60 Level Plan | 4F Plan | 3F Plan | 2F Plan | 1F Plan

HANOI'S MODEL CONDITIONS

> High density: 1,000 people/ha, the same as the existing density in 36 Streets (c.f. Amsterdam: 140 people/ha, Tokyo's central 23 wards: 150 people/ha, Hong Kong: 300 people/ha)
> Surface area of the model site: 3.3 metre wide entrance x 67 metres deep
> Low-rise: 12 metres (0-15 metres deep) to 16 metres high (depth 15 metres) according to the area's preservation code
> Porosity ratio: 50%

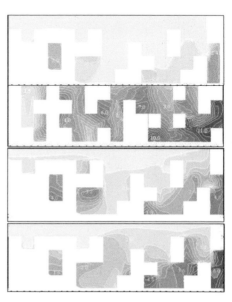

Simulation of natural ventilation and heat in porous building.

Due to legal obstacles, the team was unable to construct the prototype in 36 Streets. The prototype is currently located in the campus of the Hanoi University of Civil Engineering.

Photo collage

Grenoble, 2004

The giraffe > MATTHIEU POITEVIN

Hannibal crossed the Alps with his elephants. That's a fact. Perhaps he also stopped in Grenoble, where he was joined by a giraffe wanting to see a bit of the world. It is a matter of paying tribute to this unrecognised heroine; surely there is more merit in crossing all those mountains when you're a giraffe than if you were an elephant. *He* had mammoth ancestors genetically handing-down a kind of memorial resistance; she had nothing, but she pulled it off and no one has paid her any mind. Today, at the dawn of this new millennium, we must acknowledge her and, in the absence of the monument she deserves, create a building for her.

The campus of Pierre-Mendès University (UPMF) is characterised by an expanse of rather dull buildings, arranged as low as possible to free up the sky and engage the site.
It is nearly a minor agglomeration, yet there is nowhere for students to enjoy themselves, relax or get together. It is a place devoted to work; it is incredibly dull and used by thousands and thousands of students.
Our area of influence is bordered by the planned location of a future tramway that will bring its load of youth, thirsting for knowledge, every morning; once there, that youth will only be able to watch the grass grow and the passing clouds pose atop the mountains.
To the north and south stand two of the tallest buildings on the campus, GF+4 and +5.
It was out of the question to place the project on the ground and do away with a little more nature – that would amount to placing it in a subordinate position in relation to its neighbours, a bit like a dog on its back. Giving it great legs places it in a scale better related to its context. By freeing up the land beneath, a raised courtyard was created. This will allow everyone to chat without getting wet and serve to host temporary activities: all kinds of fairs, registration, demos, exhibitions and so on. The rest of the time, its height will let nature recover its rights. Here, the land becomes a space for ephemeral experimentation and free appropriation.

The project practically organises itself. Laid out over three levels and arranged along passageways, the building becomes as functional as possible. However, these passageways are not merely balconies for flows; they are wide and long, 4m x 28m – all it takes is the installation of a coffee or drink machine, a few garden seats, a quick cigarette, a drink or a chat, and the terraces become places of conviviality. There is no conviviality without something to drink.

The resulting façade is wrapped in a mesh of perforated stainless metal that takes its inspiration from the giraffe's spots. Anecdotes apart, this skin nuances the light and offers an interplay of urban chiaroscuro.

At night, the people circulating around the space above become Chinese shadows, and the façade comes to life, becoming an urban lampshade.

It ceases to be a façade of a building and transforms into a screen, five metres above-ground, blurring the outlines of the construction and contributing to its abstraction. It becomes the symbolic, iconographic screen that characterises the UPMF as a whole.

Here we have the result of the project, at the limit of representation; do we see what there is, or can we see other things, differently?

We are dealing with an emotional conception of architecture without the notion of façade, with a simultaneous experience of interior and exterior space, an attempt to do away with borders between inside/outside, to experience chance.

The giraffe is a silent yet spectacular animal. Anyone who's been lucky enough to get near one knows just how hard it is to see them. Despite its size and its skin, it has the ability to blend into nature and disappear.

Here where poplars and elms provide the savannah, we may add more so that this building, named LNT, is camouflaged in its environment; all the better to surprise the visitor who finally catches sight of it.

GRENOBLE. FRANCE

Client: MOU; Pierre-Mendès University, France. Represented by Hervé Castro. B.C.: Alpes Contrôle. Architects: ARM architectures, SCPA Poitevin & Reynaud. Collaborators: Mafoud Boukhalfa, Jean Lorin, Matthieu Place. Economist: Betrec. Fluids: Candotto. Electrical engineering: Ponton. Acoustics: Rouch. Main materials: Concrete, stainless metal. Surface area: 750 m². Budget: 1M €.

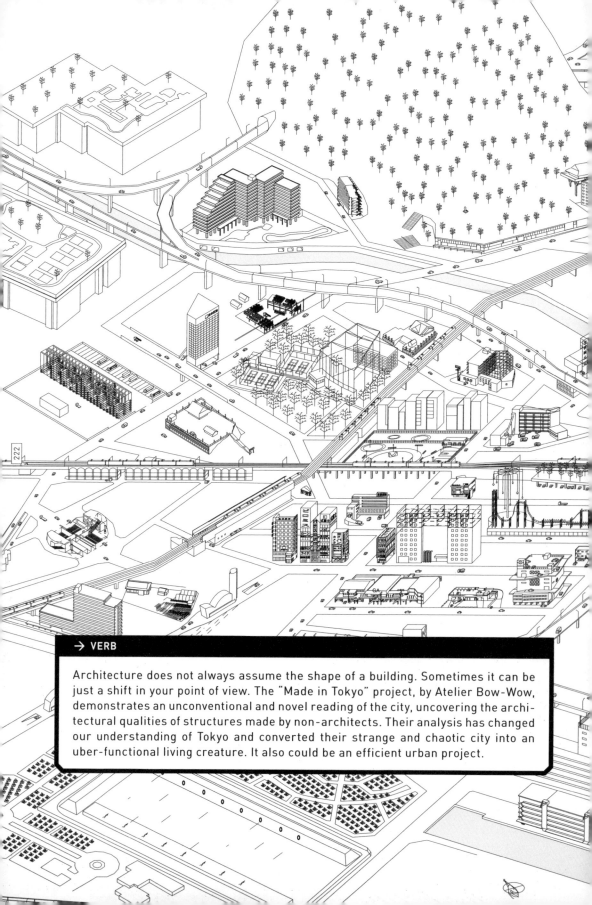

→ VERB

Architecture does not always assume the shape of a building. Sometimes it can be just a shift in your point of view. The "Made in Tokyo" project, by Atelier Bow-Wow, demonstrates an unconventional and novel reading of the city, uncovering the architectural qualities of structures made by non-architects. Their analysis has changed our understanding of Tokyo and converted their strange and chaotic city into an uber-functional living creature. It also could be an efficient urban project.

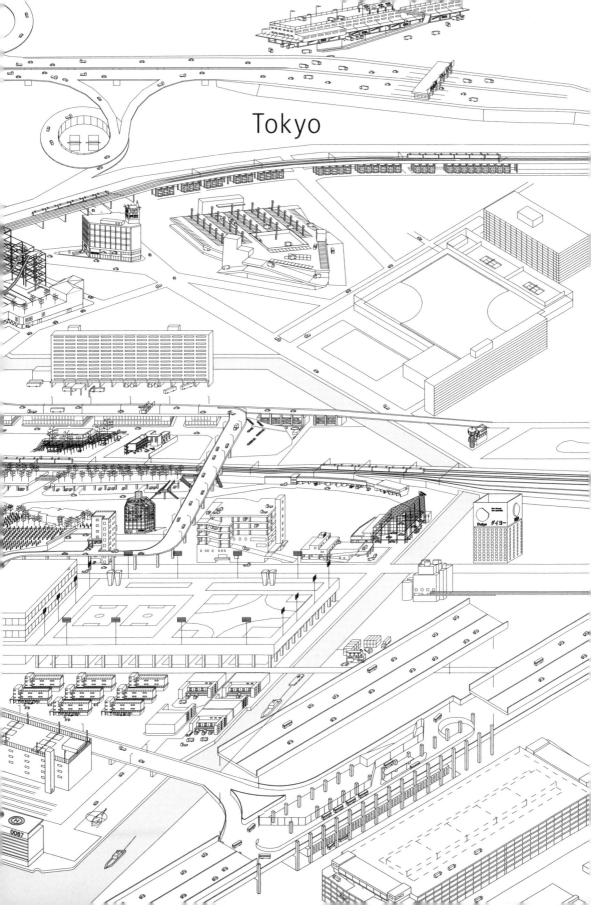

Tokyo

Made in Tokyo > Momoyo Kaijima, Yoshiharu Tsukamoto, Junzo Kuroda

"Made in Tokyo" is a series of anonymous buildings - sometimes funny, sometimes sad, sometimes too serious. Within the Tokyo Megalopolis, where so many people and things are concentrated together, these buildings result from the honest proliferation of urban situational needs. The vague, incomprehensible place called "Tokyo" somehow becomes manifest through this collection. Urbanity is directly recorded through form. Site conditions and functions can be read in this physically defined system where each single building is the harmonious union of goods, traffic, information, production, services, housing and so on. The buildings are not limited by specific power plays or architects' individual expressions: nor are they concerned with the architectural preoccupations of scale, cultural worth or history.

These stuctures appear out of greedy utilitarianism; "there is some space left over here, so lets use it for something else"; "wouldn't it be useful to put this here, and put that over there." Thus, these samples mix together with the building and the surrounding elements, yielding an unexpected and significant whole. For example, these building moments might merge together railway, roadway, retaining walls and other civil works to become something where the limit of the building becomes blurred. Another case might mix functions which are just a bit unbelievable, simply based on a similarity of the dimensional requirements of two distinct functions, or to take advantage of a thin crack of yet unused free space.

As a result, people and vehicles and objects coexist without hierarchy, occupying the same space and form, and strange new organisms of urbanism become packaged together. Each of these moments occupy a small place in Tokyo, but seem penetrated by big powers such as capitalism, social systems, and politics. They are not protected by the community from the rush of social power anymore. It might be thought that a new condition of urban-architectural space is articulated by those buildings in each specific case.

The categories of building and civil engineering, architecture and greenery start to lose their meanings, and the original reason for existence is overtaken by the coincidental meanings subsequently attached. Notions of categorization and relationships of cause and effect start to disintegrate. In thinking about the extent of architecture, we are considering architecture, which exists beyond its own framework, that can't be discussed without talking about connections to non-architectural elements; this is "Made in Tokyo".

02. Electric Passage

Several individual electronics shops fill the space below an elevated railway and train station, over a 300 m long stretch and three stories height. The arch structure, which supports the railway bridge, also serves as the arcade for the shops.
FUNCTION: Railway bridge+shopping arcade.
SITE: Sotokanda, Chiyoda-ku.

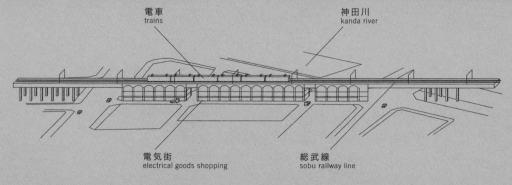

電車
trains

神田川
kanda river

電気街
electrical goods shopping

総武線
sobu railway line

07. Pachinko Cathedral

These are three separate buildings but when framed as a unit, assume the outline of Notre Dame Cathedral in Paris. Instead of bearing Biblical ornament, this Cathedral pulses with the neon lights of informational banners and advertisements announcing interior activities. The flanking towers are nearly filled with lone-shark lenders. Here we can see an ecological system in the metropolis; an endless cycle of losing money at pachinko, borrowing money from a lone shark, losing money...

FUNCTION: Pachinko parlour + lone-shark 'bank.'
SITE: Kabuki-cho, Shinjuku.

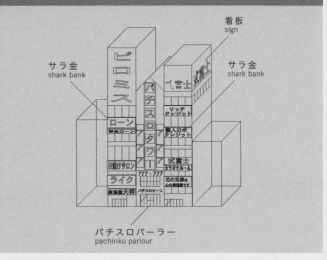

看板
sign

サラ金
shark bank

サラ金
shark bank

パチスロパーラー
pachinko parlour

46. Apartment Mountain Temple

The Konpira Shrine sits adjacent an apartment building. The internal staircase and roof of the apartment now become the path of religious procession. The forecourt of the temple is covered with waterproof sheeting instead of pebbles or gravel.

FUNCTION: Buddhist temple + private apartment house.
SITE: Daimachi, Hodogaya-ku, Yokohama-shi.

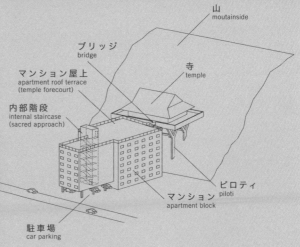

山
moutainside

ブリッジ
bridge

寺
temple

マンション屋上
apartment roof terrace
(temple forecourt)

内部階段
internal staircase
(sacred approach)

ピロティ
piloti

マンション
apartment block

駐車場
car parking

Pet Architecture Project >
Atelier Bow-Wow + Tokyo Institute of Technology, Tsukamoto Architectural Lab.

Pets are small, humorous and charming. We have found instances of "Pet Architectures," which are also small, humorous and charming, located in various spots throughout Tokyo. They occupy surprisingly small sites: 1m-wide gap between the buildings in highly built-up areas, tiny subdivided swatch of land, or a long and thin block sliced by roads and railroads, remenants of various and distinct stages of city planning. These small structures, larger than a doghouse and smaller than a building, can be considered the "Pet" of city space. This is the project of "Pet Architecture".

32. Tobacco Shop

Four vending machines: one for drinks, a pay phone, one for cigarettes and a mailbox constituting a complete set of "urban" appliances, lined up in the setback space of a condominium building. Available are 177 push bottons to choose from: 68 for drinks, 97 for cigarette and 12 for calling. The owner of this condomimium dreams of having a small tobacco shop to replace of these machines in the future.
SIZE: 1.1 x 1.8 x 2.2
SITE: Higashigotanda, Shinagawa-ku.

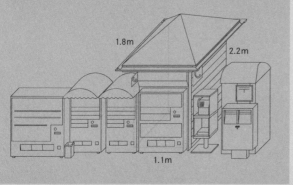

46. Kadokko

An eatery located between an old street and newer loop road. There is a door for customers entering from the road, a door into the kitchen from the street and a steel staircase leading up to the private residence at the corner. Standing on the top of the stair, you feel like you are starring in "Titanic", where the entire city block transformed into a luxury cruise liner, until the toilet below and air conditioner unit interrupt the fantasy.
USE: Restaurant.
SIZE: 4.8 x 0.9 x 6.2
SITE: Wakabayashi, Setagaya-ku.

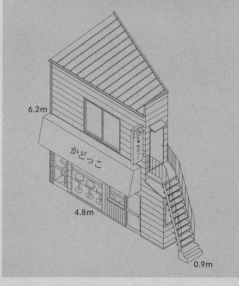

62. Bikebox Ikebukuro

This motorbike shop is 39 m long and is located in a trianglular site, formed by the construction of the Kawagoe Kaido Highway. At its thinnest, the wedge-shaped building measures only 20 cm and is used for posting advertisements. From there the building grows to house the showroom, the office and finally at its widest, the 6 m wide repair shop. In the showroom, the moterbikes are organized in ascending size, from minibikes up to the 750 cc bikes.

USE: Moterbike shop.
SIZE: 39 x 0.2 x 4.5
SITE: Honmachi, Shibuya-ku.

77. Mini House

The site of the Mini House faces a road, private path and open field, future site of a new roadway. Thus the architects decided to design the house with no back face. Unlike the surrounding houses, this house has no fence. A cube was placed in the center of this site, and sub volumes containing the entrance, kitchen and bathroom jut out in different directions, taking advantage of certain views. The floor is half a level higher than the ground, shifting the eye-level of the inhabitants slightly above that of the closely situated next-door neighbours.

Designed by Atelier Bow-Wow
SIZE: 3.7 x 1.5 x 3.7
SITE: Nerima-ku.

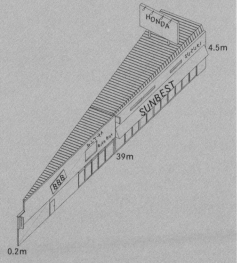

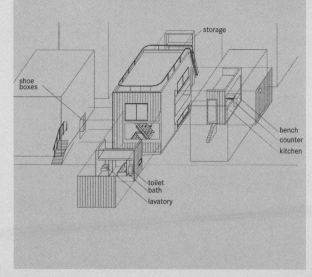

Small houses made in Tokyo

A conversation between Momoyo Kaijima and Yoshiharu Tsukamoto
Atelier Bow-Wow

THE SOCIAL NATURE OF PRIVATE HOUSES

Yoshiharu Tsukamoto (YT) Although Tokyo is recognized as a dense city, its population density is in fact, low. On average the city is blanketed by 1.5-story buildings. Thus, much of Tokyo is occupied by individual homes and the sheer number of building lots and houses is extremely high. Visually it is very dense. Tokyo has building density rather than population density. Within this situation, we are rethinking the 'behavior of houses.'

Momoyo Kaijima (MK) Whereas in Europe collective housing is more prevalent, here in Japan the majority of the population live in free-standing, individual houses. In this sense, Tokyo is composed of individual housing units that we consider capable of being treated as social elements.

YT In a dense area of Tokyo, designing a house within lot limits without also taking into account the surrounding housing context does not make sense. Imagine a typical ocurrance where collective apartments are built among individual houses. Because "facing south" is greatly valued in Japan, one would first construct a house that opens to a garden located to the south and circulation to the north. Soon afterwards, an apartment building is built in the adjacent plot to the south and suddenly the new neighbors, circulating along the common corridor, become the backdrop to the once private garden of the individual house. This juxtaposition generates privacy conflicts and the "perfect plan," one circumscribed within its lot, becomes absurd when considered with respect to neighboring buildings. Starting with the typical condition of a 70 m^2 plot with a 50% built-up area, it is extremely difficult to design a house that relates well to its neighbouring buildings. Urban planning is not concerned with the designs ocurring inside individual lots. It generally imposes rules over an entire area, while most buildings are designed to best take advantage of individual lot conditions. This means that architecture never connects to the city. We are reconsidering the way in which houses situate themselves in the city, in order to make connections between them.

HOW TO USE TOKYO

YT Our clients use Tokyo to live. Here, 'Tokyo' is not a entirety, but part of different areas of functions and activities. For example, in our DAS HOUSE project, the clients work in Hatsudai and often go to the Fuchu Race Track for leisure. They purchased a plot for their house at the midpoint between these activities, which are connected by the Keio Railway Line. In this case, Tokyo becomes a 'cut-out' of the Keio Line. If you do not manage all your activities efficiently, it is possible to waste a significant amount of time and then become stressed. A house can be a tool to help create a 'cut-out' area of Tokyo.

MK Many of our clients choose their plot by first thinking about how they will use Tokyo. They elect to purchase a plot within the area along the specifc train line which best connects their network of activites. The house acts as an edited city in their mind. They are less interested in the house as a status symbol and more interested in how it might be used in their customization of the city.

YT ...or simply they love their area, without judging their locale as the most useful area in the context of their various experiences. One day they began living in one area and continue to live in the same place for three, five, or ten years. Thus gradually, they come to develop their own specificity in that area.

MK People today have learned to be critical towards the city of Tokyo. They carefully observe the city in order to see where to live or how the area works. By saying 'I feel good in this area' or 'I don't think it's very comfortable to live here', they judge the place.

YT The clients of our generation regard the choice of area with high priority. They say 'we want to live in this area of the city' rather than 'we want to live in this type of location.' It appears that they are 'outsourcing' many of their everyday activities beyond the physical limits of their houses and perceive a clear connection between interior and exterior.

INSIDE OF A STREET

YT Surrounding conditions have a tremendous effect on design. Some residential districts are defined by the qualities of a collective atmosphere or 'interior intimacy' created by neighboring houses. Although we have yet to enter a particular home, we somehow understand that we have entered 'inside,' having crossed a threshold. In such places you can still see some common rules that all the local neighbors practice during the maintainance of their place. This is something that brings us back to the way old villages and markets were organized. The character of this type of 'interior space' has been disappearing from Japan since the introduction of modern architecture. I think we have to recreate this type of 'insideness,' which is independent from conventional communities. The problem is that these rules usually develop over long periods of time, which make them an unreasonable and absurd restriction in the context of today's constantly changing society. In this sense, such rules and common practices were seen as outdated and undesirable during modernization and the period of high economic growth. In our view, architects of the preceeding generation, those who we respect, have treated these rules in such a manner.

Now, architects should make strategic use of the value of these rules in the creation of city space cultures. Because Japan is a country of few resources, tourism, design, and the service industry have become very important areas of our economy. The city composed of private houses is very interesting in itself, but is currently insufficient as a city culture worth visiting by tourists. In the future, tourism could be more about what is unique in each place. It will be much more interesting to see what is happening now, or how people manage their present space, rather than visiting a historic site.

MK What you mean is that design can be a matter of constant communication, where thinking about architecture and thinking about the city invariably occur simultaneously and simbiotically.

A HOUSE AND A NEW WAY OF LIFE

MK I feel that our clients also want to try to live a 'new way of life' in Tokyo.

YT Clients vary as much as do the sites. Some remain unmarried, some do not have children, some have two incomes, and some work at home. They have very different lifestyles from residents of a typical suburban house built during the period of high economic growth.

MK Until recently this diversity was described in terms of a crisis, where the 'collapse of the traditional family' had lead to 'changes in the community.' However, our clients are simply the product of this shift and do not have these negative feelings.

YT We feel that the clients and the sites vary a lot, really, in spite of the fact that their size and price fall more or less within the same range. In this situation, what we, the architect, should do is...

MK ...offer an alternative to a stereotypical solution. Clients want a house that is designed for a certain site and based on their own specific interests and not on abstractions. Architects respond to the demands of individual and social needs through the design of private houses.

YT There is the premise that the character of the site and of the clients are unique to each case, but through the making of every house, we would also like to raise other questions which go beyond those based on individual interests. I think that one of the reasons why people chose to build a house is that they can paint it or change it over time as they like. The desire to have a house is transforming into the desire to voluntary engage with a space – clients are designing the space by themselves or combining interesting elements they find somewhere.

MK If we think of our basic needs – food, clothing and shelter – we often cook what we eat and we choose what we wear from various styles and price range, but we don't have the same amount of freedom regarding where we live.

YT We have little experience regarding living conditions. When it comes to space we are very passive and have little choice. We cannot decide to live in this house tomorrow and live in another house the day after tomorrow. I think it is significant that we cannot judge a house from experience. But at least now, we have knowledge about houses from magazines and books.

MK Yes, we are surrounded by more and more information.

YT This means that the way in which houses are perceived and defined has been changing. In the period of high economic growth, only rich or educated people asked architects to design their houses, and at that time, design theory dominated the significance of space.
Today clients have more choices when they think about their new home. They may opt to renovate their old house, join a housing cooperative, or take part in the design of a new house via an intense communication with the architects. The significance of space does not only mean design, but also refers to the ability of designing or building things by oneself, making use of old materials, or deciding that living space can mix with work space.

MK Sometimes our clients tell us that they would like the design of their house to serve as an instructive example of a new way of living.

YT That's right. As we architects want to create works in alternative ways, clients also want to live in alternative ways.

MK And what they expect from architects is technical assitance or advice about how to realize their house. That's what they ask of professional designers of architecture.

YT Yes, I think so.

MK And that's why more and more architects say that designing a house is a collaboration with the clients.

YT In that sense, it is communication rather than collaboration.

MK Yes, architecture is an art that opens up many possibilities to a set of problems...

YT ...or means to occupy space, or a form of spatial media...

MK If we define architecture as a spatial medium, where the autonomy of the dwellers is expressed, then what is the role of design? If we only try to make practical space, then we might say that design doesn't matter anymore. All that clients need would be an easy-to-use space.

YT The best thing would be that everybody could design architecture.

MK But...

YT We would get caught up in cliches very often. Except for some extraordinary person or condition, it is very difficult to make something freely without falling into cliches. If architects tend to produce cliches, then even more so non-professionals.

MK Then how can we escape from that?

YT We can go back to zero. Cliches are caused by certain practices that repeat solutions. But the essential quality of design is to start from zero in each case and then to test: 'if we combine these two things together, that will happen,' or 'by doing this we can solve this problem and that problem together'. We can thus change the notion of space as practical into one that is truly experiencial. Of course 'zero' is an extreme way to phrase things, and we have to have both respect for and a critical understanding of the rules and culture established throughout the history of housing design.

LAYOUT THE THINGS

MK When we start to design a house, we ask the clients to describe their needs and the way they live. We ask things like: 'do you sleep on a futon or in a bed? Do you have a piano or not?' because one of the ways to make a small house is to layout the things the clients already have.

YT And abandoning the standard 'nLDK' method, which is the common layout of a house or flat with an [n number of bedrooms + living room + dining room + kitchen], helps our design process. In Japan, where space is very limited and dimensions are extremely tight, the layout or positioning of a client's things will also affect how the client, himself is positioned in the house.

MK In this sense, a house with traditional tatami mats is very interesting. Tatami mats have held a very important role in the spatial flexibility of a house. You can bring in furniture to give the space a functional definition, or you can put down a futon to make it a sleeping room. A similar approach is to build a shelf-wall that can link or divide spaces depending upon on whether the shelves are full or not. In this way floors, walls, or shelves function as infrastructure.

YT The houses we design are not divided into individual rooms according to the nLDK format but connected like a string with some spatial fragmentations. We think that this character of 'connected but fragmented' is important in a modern urban house.

DESIGNING TIME

MK I recently started to consider the importance of time, in the sense of spatial growth or development. Here the term 'time,' refers to a manner of sustaining the house, or to specific ways of spend time in it.

YT But if we talk about the concept of a 'lived-in house,' in the sense that its inhabitants create such a space over time, we, as architects, cannot do that. By investing time and energy, any space can become a 'lived-in house.' Thus, it appears that there cannot exist a feedback process between such a space and our design activity. Therefore, we have to look for others ways of getting some type of feedback from time.
Maybe we can treat time as a practical level of sustainability, or as an element in spatial perception. I mean that while we cannot design with time, we can try to engage it through environmental or material derivation.

MK We have to think about the whole house, not about specific details. Space can be realized by the intent to use it, not only by concrete functions. Thus an analysis, or reading of the clients' intentions regarding the use of the building, is necessary. Our 'Made in Tokyo' project can be understood as the 'lived-in house' reading of the buildings. Hmm... but in the case of 'Made in Tokyo', we made a kind of 'fictional' reading, which could be interpreted as a form of 'design that intervenes in the process'. Don't you think so?

From the book *Semakute Chiisai Tanoshii Ie* (A Tiny, Small and Happy House) by Akira Nagae + Atelier Bow-Wow, Hara Shobou Publishers, 2004.

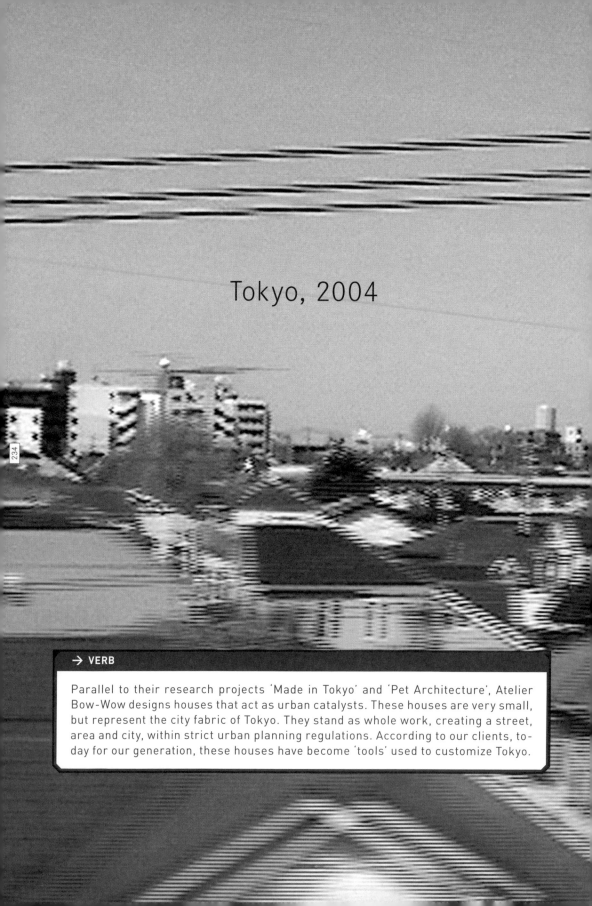

Tokyo, 2004

→ **VERB**

Parallel to their research projects 'Made in Tokyo' and 'Pet Architecture', Atelier Bow-Wow designs houses that act as urban catalysts. These houses are very small, but represent the city fabric of Tokyo. They stand as whole work, creating a street, area and city, within strict urban planning regulations. According to our clients, to-day for our generation, these houses have become 'tools' used to customize Tokyo.

Setagaya-ku

Architect Yoshiharu Tsukamoto visits the house. ↑
Client welcomes him from the entrance
1.5 m above the ground.

The clients Mr. and Mrs Nagae. Akira Nagae ←
(left) is journalist, and finally made a
documentary book about this GAE house
from his viewpoint as a client.

From the book *Semakute Chiisai Tanoshii Ie* (A Tiny,
Small and Happy House) by Akira Nagae + Atelier
Bow-Wow, Hara Shobou Publishers, 2004.

236

GAE House > Atelier Bow-Wow

Named after the clients, Mr. and Mrs. NAGAE, the GAE-house was designed in two different sites. The first GAE house was sited in Jiyugaoka, next to a park. The building conditions were very restrictive, so naturally the roof responded to setback regulations and the
structure has three floors with a wooden frame. Because the property was to be leased,
only wooden buildings were permitted by law. Mr. and Mrs Nagae chose this lot because
they were familar with the area of Jiyugaoka, taking many walks and shopping at the same
second-hand bookstore for over ten years. This first project was halted due to a problem in
aquiring the land lease and subsequently moved to another site in neighbouring Okusawa.
Okusawa is a very old residential area that still retains a nice continuity of natural, green
fencing. The lot is only 85 m², with a mere six or seven meters of the perimeter facing
the street. Thus, placing the client's car in front of the house excluded the possibility of
maintaining the natural fence. Instead we shifted its location from front of the house and
planted the fence to one side and to the back, so as to "continue" it. The main volume of
the house was placed in the center, with a big roof with a 1 m deep soffit, designed to take
advantage of the fact that eaves are not included in building-to-land ratio. The front of the
house has a 2 m overhang, which creates just enough room to accommodate the client's
car. The roof soffit is also made of transparent glass, designed to bring in the maximum
levels of indirect light. From the exterior, the house appears to be a two- storey building,
but in reality has three interior floors.

Mr. and Ms. Nagae had a very clear way of living, which we tried to maintain in the building's design. Each floor has a different function and interior surface: a metal deck at the
top level, white flooring in the middle level and wooden flooring below. The middle floor
is displaced a half level up from ground level and contains the entrance, bathroom and
sunroom. The semi-buried ground floor houses the study and bedroom. The upper floor is
almost completely covered by the metal deck of the peaked roof. Mr. Nagae is a journalist,
who works at home, and has a tremendous library. The downstairs bookshelves, 50 meters
in total length, form the interior finish of the basement floor. Though this level lacks windows, it is not covered by a ceiling and receives natural light, reflected in from the white
flooring of the level above.

← Client Miyoko Nagae standing under
the stairs. To help light pass through
the stairwell, the wooden floor at this
level is painted completely white.

← Architect Tsukamoto washes his hands.

hedge

setback regulation
from road width

attic

mashroom shape
made by setback regulation

1.25

1

horizontal band window

sun room

office at home

→ Looking study from bedroom

↓ Bedroom.
Natural wood finish.

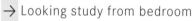

← Looking to the study room below

↘ Looking up to the entrance
2 bicycles are hanged on the wall

↑ Looking down to study from entrance.
A wall finish of books and shelves.
The total collection measures 50m long.

← The study is also the client's office.

← Client looks up to the top-side-light with shading system, horizontal window.

GAE HOUSE, SETAGAYA-KU, TOKYO. JAPAN

Client: Akira Nagae + Miyoko Nagae. Design: Atelier Bow-Wow. Project architects: Momoyo Kaijima, Yoshiharu Tsukamoto, Junzo Kuroda. Structure: steel frame. Site area: 79.37 m². Building area: 36.32 m². Total floor area: 88.42 m².

← Entrance. Architect puts his shoes on.

↖ Looking down to the entrance from dining room.

Architect and clients look down at the garden from horizontal, soffit window.

View of dining table from kitchen space.

View of horizontal soffit windows from below into second floor dining room
Piping located wall in wall, at triangular section
↓

Mitaka-shi

DAS House > Atelier Bow-Wow

The site of the DAS House was chosen because it lies between the client's hobby place (race track) and his workplace. This small house has a central stair-core that acts like a spine connecting all the rooms, which are organized around the core and may be separated by sliding doors. Initially, the bedroom was located on the ground floor and the living room, kitchen, and work space on the second. However, once the clients adopted a second pet, they decided to change the room layout. The bed was moved upstairs and the sofa was put downstairs, allowing the dogs more freedom. The walls are lined with shelves, which when customized with things, allow the adjacent spaces to be more defined. For instance, the shelf next to the kitchen contains plates and glasses to help form a dining and the shelf next to the entrance has books and toys to help form a room for living. This space also has two windows lined with a mirror to create reflections of the sky and views of the ground.

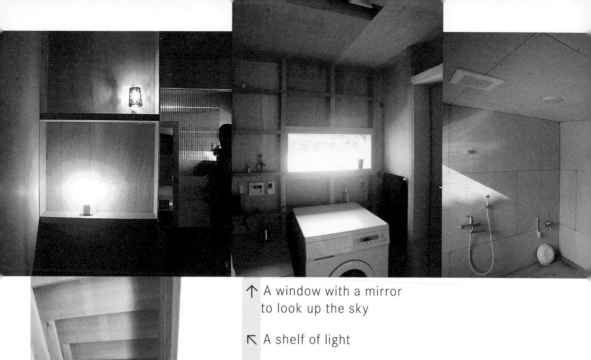

↑ A window with a mirror
  to look up the sky

↖ A shelf of light

↗ Shower room

← Restroom under the stairs
  with auto-open cover

↑ Central staircase. All rooms
  are connected to this core

← Diaphanous curtain

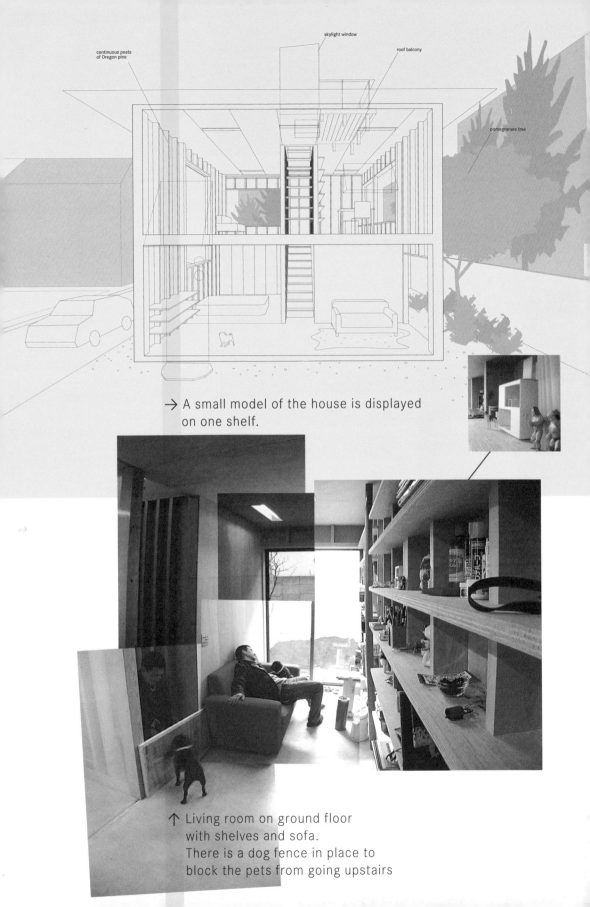

continuous posts
of Oregon pine

skylight window

roof balcony

pomegranate tree

→ A small model of the house is displayed
on one shelf.

↑ Living room on ground floor
with shelves and sofa.
There is a dog fence in place to
block the pets from going upstairs

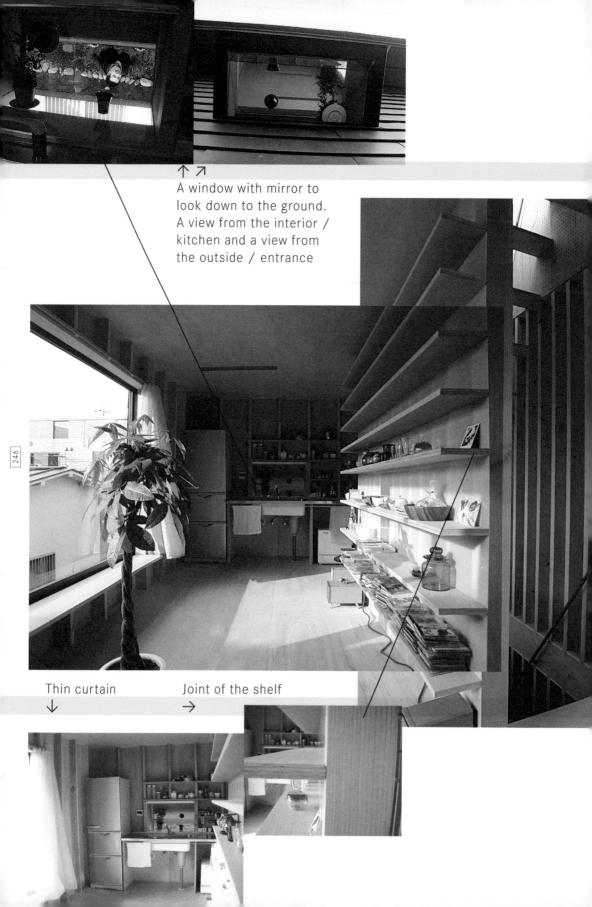

A window with mirror to
look down to the ground.
A view from the interior /
kitchen and a view from
the outside / entrance

246

Thin curtain

Joint of the shelf

Kitchen range can be covered
to be continuous to the cooking table

↑

DAS HOUSE, MITAKA-SHI, TOKYO. JAPAN

Design: Atelier Bow-Wow. <u>Project architects</u>: Momoyo Kaijima, Yoshiharu Tsukamoto, Junzo Kuroda. <u>Structure</u>: wood.
<u>Site area</u>: 94.46 m². <u>Building area</u>: 36 m². <u>Total floor area</u>: 74 m².

Working space
on the back of the stairs
↓

Sliding doors
are opened
and closed
↖ ↑

Architect Yoshiharu
Tsukamoto and
the clients' dog
↓

Shanghai, 2002

→ VERB

Those two projects in Shanghai and Niigata, are designed for exhibitions of contemporary art. They are not objects to watch, but equipments to serve for local people. After the investigation in those cities, they picked up customes on the street and re-made its culture in the form of moving architecture. At a glance they look peculiar, but everybody knows how it works. These are micro portable equipments for the city to connect the people.

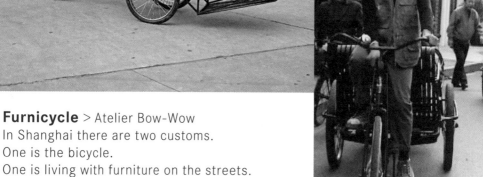

Furnicycle > Atelier Bow-Wow
In Shanghai there are two customs.
One is the bicycle.
One is living with furniture on the streets.
Today's urban development eliminates those.
That is pity.
The idea of living in the city streets and not a house is wonderful.
We combine these customs and make a new custom.

On the street
↓

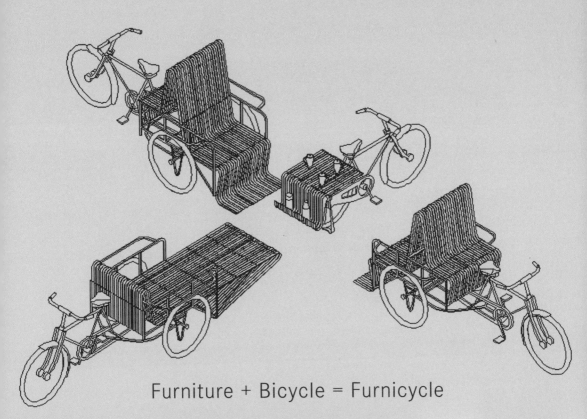

Furniture + Bicycle = Furnicycle

At Shanghai Art Museum
↓

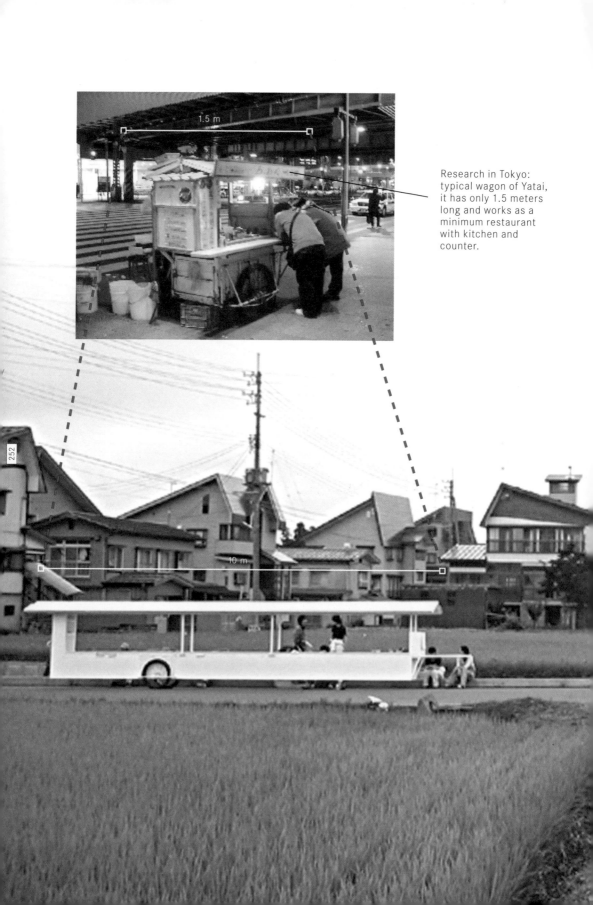

1.5 m

Research in Tokyo:
typical wagon of Yatai,
it has only 1.5 meters
long and works as a
minimum restaurant
with kitchen and
counter.

10 m

White Limousine Yatai Project > Atelier Bow-Wow
"Yatai" is the very popular Japanese open-air restaurant style that is the wagon moving and staying in the street, serving the guest with food and drinks. Normally it is 1.5m long. But we enlarge it to 10m long as making micro public space in the town.
In the winter Tokaimachi City has a lot of snow that is making strong character of this area, but in this summer art exhibition people could not see the snow. So we painted it white and restaurant menu served only white food and drinks for the people who are thinking about the snow.

Tokaimachi, Niigata, 2003

Model: stretch a wagon of Yatai to 10m long limousine, and paint completely white. It has mini kitchen and long long table to eat with many people.

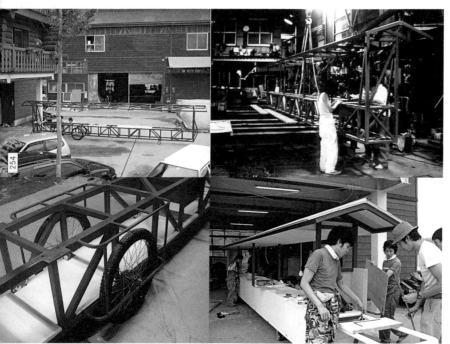

254

Structure

Furnishing

Under Construction / Kanetake
Construction 7-14 July 2003

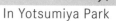
In Yotsumiya Park

Roof drain detail

←

↑
Roof

↙
Anchor

↓
Wheel for bicycle

Tofu, jiao-zi, rice, rice cake, ice shavings, sake... white and transparent foods and drinks are served in white plates and bowls, to imagine the snowy winter of this area
↓

Rent o the town event
↓

←

Before and after

↑
Parade of Kimono Nagashi

The White Limousine Yatai went to parks, event, parade...

Verb connection is the third volume of Actar's boogazine.
It was edited by Albert Ferré, Irene Hwang, Michael Kubo, Ramon Prat, Tomoko Sakamoto, Jaime Salazar, Catherine Szacka, and Anna Tetas, with graphic design by David Lorente, translations by Elaine Fradley and the collaboration of everyone here at Actar. Printed by Ingoprint and distributed by our in-house representatives.
Our thanks to all authors whose generous contribution of ideas and materials has made this issue possible. In addition, this publication has relied on the invaluable collaboration of Sawako Akune, Michael Bell, Mads Boserup Lauritsen, Esteve Fornells, Iker Gil, Deborah Jacobs, Yuzo Kariya, Iao Katagiri, Judy Lewis, Cynni Murphy, Daisuke Sanuki, Shun Takagi, Marco van Middelkoop, Yuryu.

Contact info:
ACTAR
Roca i Batlle 2
E-08023 Barcelona
www.actar.es
phone +34 934 187 759
fax +34 934 186 707
verb@actar-mail.com

Distribution:
info@actar-mail.com

ISBN 84-95951-06-1
DL B-50.336-2004
Printed and bound in the European Union
Barcelona, December 2004